Advance Praise for *The Oth*

"This story stands as a perfect example to teams at all levels of the power of persistence, the importance of players accepting their roles, and the rewards that result when everyone agrees upon a common goal."

—Mike Miller, two-time NBA champion, winner of the NBA's Rookie of the Year and Sixth Man of the Year Awards, and Houston High School (TN) boys basketball head coach

"An inspiring story of struggle and sacrifice that every high school athlete and coach can relate to, *The Other Side of Glory* will be a favorite for generations to come."

—Rocky Ford, basketball chair, Texas Girls Coaches Association

"I've been coaching high school basketball for over 20 years and this is exactly the type of book I look for. Carl Pierson captures the roller coaster ride that we all endure while coaching high school hoops. I sincerely enjoyed reading this inspiring true story!"

—Dori Oldaker, head coach of USA Basketball's 2016 U17 world championship team and five-time Pennsylvania state champion Mt. Lebanon High School

"Carl Pierson does an excellent job capturing the essence of coaching high school basketball. The Other Side of Glory is highly accurate in its portrayal of the ups and downs of high school athletics."

—Jeremey Finn, 2020 Ohio State High School Basketball Coaches Association coach of the year

"Carl Pierson deftly chronicles the in-depth journey of a girls high school basketball season. He paints this picture with a beautiful brush and vivid detail, highlighting the different personalities that will inspire any true lover of the game. As a basketball coach of 43 years, I thoroughly recommend this book."

—Doc Scheppler, coach of six California high school state championship teams and head coach at Pinewood High School (CA)

"The path to success is so very seldom linear. *The Other Side of Glory* is a perfect reminder that behind every success story are miles and miles of failures and struggles, but with dedication and belief, you can accomplish anything no matter where you started. A needed reminder that in a time where instant gratification seemingly rules, the long, winding journey is really what it's all about."

—Blake DuDonis, head women's basketball coach, University of Wisconsin–River Falls

"This book should be required reading for every parent and high school basketball player. It captures the very essence of high school basketball. Combine that with examples, failures, successes, and situations that every program will experience at some point, and you have a book that will become a basketball doctrine. Carl Pierson has done it again."

—Greg White, West High School (Centerton, AR)

THE
OTHER SIDE
OF GLORY

THE OTHER SIDE OF GLORY

A Team's Quest for High School Girls Basketball History

CARL J. PIERSON

TRIUMPH
BOOKS

Library of Congress Cataloging-in-Publication Data available upon request.

This book is available in quantity at special discounts for your group or organization. For further information, contact:

Triumph Books LLC
814 North Franklin Street
Chicago, Illinois 60610
(312) 337-0747
www.triumphbooks.com

Printed in U.S.A.
ISBN: 978-1-62937-923-4
Design by Patricia Frey

Dedicated to Colton and to all the kids buried at the end of the bench who never get their names in the newspaper but continue to do all they can to contribute to the success of their team.

Contents

Foreword

It is with tremendous honor that I write the foreword for *The Other Side of Glory*. Growing up 35 miles from Waconia in Hutchinson, Minnesota, I understand the pride the student-athletes on the Waconia team played with for their hometown. Never making it to the state tournament myself as a high school basketball player but achieving success later in my playing career, I appreciate what these players were able to accomplish.

The chapter "Always the Bridesmaid" brought me back to the first decade or so of my playing career. As I mentioned, I did not make it to state in high school, instead losing in the section finals in three of my high school seasons. In college at Minnesota I found more success, and yet even the year when we went to the Final Four, we lost to the University of Connecticut in the semifinals. After my college career, I was drafted by the Connecticut Sun of the WNBA in 2004. We went to the WNBA Finals my first two seasons with the franchise and lost both times. I truly began to wonder if I would always finish second, always be the bridesmaid.

In January 2010 I was traded back to my home-state franchise, the Minnesota Lynx. Many things fell into place at the right time. I joined the team in the same season as the WNBA's all-time leading rebounder Rebekkah Brunson. All-Star Seimone Augustus was coming off a knee injury and was nearly back to 100 percent. In 2011 the Lynx drafted Maya Moore, and Taj McWilliams-Franklin was signed as a free agent. Having great players coupled with hard work and a Hall of Fame coach in Cheryl Reeve, we were able to create a dynasty, winning four championships in seven years. I was also able to achieve success on a world level, winning four gold medals for USA Basketball over an eight-year stretch: two Olympic gold medals and two World Championship gold medals.

Through my journey, there were "Dark Decembers" and an "All of Us" mentality along the way. Eventually some would say I found glory and something close to what the Waconia team felt when they were "Immortals." My journey and the journey of the Waconia girls basketball team shows us that if you persevere through adversity, stick together as a team, work through conflict, and have passion for the game you love, then anything is possible.

—Lindsay Whalen

Head coach, University of Minnesota women's basketball

CHAPTER 1

20 Seconds

This time was going to be different.

Everyone in the arena could sense it.

Even though an enormous number of Waconia High School's 1,200 students were absent, (having made their annual spring break escape to bask on warm beaches), the noise generated by the crowd made it sound as though everyone who remained in the town of 12,000 people had made the ten-mile drive to Chanhassen to cheer on their Wildcats in the section championship game.

Even the defending state champion Cooper Hawks were beginning to gather that this time would be different. To their great surprise, Cooper had found themselves trailing to the lower-seeded Wildcats for most of the game. The Cooper players had adopted a glassy-eyed, deer-in-the-headlights stare. The Hawks sat on the state's basketball throne, and they had fully expected Waconia would bend the knee. When Cooper finally recognized the Wildcats would do no such thing, time was rapidly running out.

A final, frantic rally by the defending champs had lifted them into the lead by a single point with one minute to play. But the Wildcats and their loyal fans, who had seen the team come so painfully close so many times, were undeterred. This time was going to be different.

Moments after Cooper claimed their narrow lead, a Waconia junior guard called Snake by her coaches lived up to her nickname. As the Hawks embarked on an effort to protect their newfound lead, the Cooper point guard attempted a pass and Snake struck with the quickness of a cobra, snatching the ball out of the air before it reached its intended target. An instant later she saw a teammate streaking down the floor and fired a long pass ahead of her. A freshman referred to as Raptor converted the uncontested layup. Suddenly the Wildcats were back up by one and the Waconia side of the gym erupted in excitement.

Cooper came up empty on their next possession. The Wildcats had the ball back and a one-point lead with 35 seconds left. Cooper had only been whistled for four fouls to that point in the second half, though Waconia fans would tell you the officials had ignored several more. The Hawks would need to foul three more times before they could force the Wildcats to the free-throw line. As precious seconds continued to vanish from the clock, it was evident the Cooper players failed to recognize the need to foul. Waconia was quite content to dribble around, knowing that with each subsequent tick of the clock, they were inching ever closer to a spot in the state tournament. The defending state champion

Hawks had been so dominant for so long, it seemed they had forgotten what to do when losing late in a game.

After more dribbling and delay by the Wildcats, the ball found its way to Waconia's junior point guard and cocaptain, a player they called Bird. She held the ball out near halfcourt, content to allow the clock to continue its steady march toward zero. Cooper's coaches were jumping and yelling franticly on the far sideline, attempting to attract the attention of their team. When the Hawks finally noticed their coaches engaged in what looked like calisthenics, the message was instantly understood. The Hawks had to foul. The Cooper defender closest to Bird amped up her pressure, stabbing at the ball with explosive precision, moving in a blur. Waconia's savvy point guard managed to stay a fraction of a second ahead of the assault, maneuvering the ball away just barely beyond the defender's reach.

Then, in an attempt to avoid being called for a five-second violation, Bird plunged the ball against the light brown wood floor and dribbled down the lane toward the basket. As Bird drove, her defender's feet got tangled. The Cooper player tripped and fell to the ground. Dribbling at full speed, Bird was not able to avoid the defender suddenly sprawled out directly in front of her. Bird collided with the fallen defender and she quickly crumpled to the ground. Every fan in the arena anxiously anticipated the whistle that would signal a foul.

But the whistle never sounded. Instead, in the aftermath of the bodies hitting the hardwood, the ball bounced away from Bird and rolled out of bounds. Rather than raising his hand in a fist to signal the foul that seemed so obvious to all, the nearest official stopped the clock with a short, loud tweet then dramatically pointed in the direction of Cooper's basket. The Waconia fans responded with ferocity. Despite their hostile shouts and aggressive gestures, the defending champions would be awarded the ball and a final chance to defend their title with 20 seconds left. Cooper took a timeout.

When the Wildcats gathered at the bench, their coach—his voice hoarse from yelling over the din of the crowd—shouted, "You are one stop away from the state tournament!" With the miniscule amount of time remaining, the Wildcats needed just one more steal, one more rebound. There were at least a dozen other ways the closing seconds could play out in their favor. For Waconia it didn't matter how it happened; they just had to keep Cooper from scoring one more time. If they did, the Wildcats would secure the first state tournament appearance in the 45-year history of the program.

The contrasts between Cooper and Waconia were stark and numerous. Cooper was one of two huge high schools in a large suburban school district just west of Minneapolis. Cooper had been in Minnesota's largest class (AAAA) with a 9th- through 12th-grade enrollment of about 1,700 students. However, because such a large percentage of those 1,700 kids came from lower socioeconomic situations and qualified for free and reduced lunch, the state high school league had a formula that allowed Cooper to move down to Class AAA. The year before, Cooper petitioned to make the move, and they coasted to the Class AAA state championship.

As recently as 2000, Waconia was a small rural town of 7,000 people. Located 35 miles southwest of Minneapolis, Waconia had no major highways or interstates running through it. For that reason, the town had been a hidden gem. Early in the new millennium, as the Twin Cities' suburbs continued to creep further into the countryside, families looked further west, and Waconia was no longer a secret. Thousands of upper-income families built huge new homes in the town because of its location and its large, beautiful lake. During this decade of robust growth, the number of students at Waconia High School tripled from 400 to nearly 1,200. Unlike at Cooper, the number of kids who qualified for free and reduced lunch was almost nonexistent. Cooper had descended from AAAA due to difficult economic conditions and their success in Class AAA was immediate. The Wildcats ascended from Minnesota's small school class as the city grew from an influx of affluence, and after two decades in Class AAA, the Wildcats' list of near-misses and heartbreaking finishes was long.

None of that mattered now as both teams huddled around their respective coaches to devise the strategy for the game's closing seconds. On the Waconia bench there was deliberation: Cooper was a team of talented guards, adept at slashing and driving to the basket. Should the Wildcats revert back to the 2-3 zone that had given the Hawks so much trouble for most of the game? Or was it wiser to play person-to-person defense in an effort to make it more difficult for the Hawks to get an easy open shot? The players expressed their support for person-to-person and their coach was comfortable with the rationale. He also admired the confidence and the conviction the players expressed when proclaiming their preference.

The Wildcats exited the huddle one strong defensive possession away from the goal that had eluded the hundreds of players that had put on the purple-and-gold uniforms before them. Twenty ticks of the clock were all that separated Waconia from the state tournament.

The Wildcats fans roared in unison as Cooper passed the ball in from the sideline near halfcourt. It was clear the crowd was intent on doing everything it could to distract the Hawks and help their defenders in the final seconds. Cooper's point guard couldn't call out a play over the noise of the fans, so she hoisted up her left hand to signal her team. Then she dribbled to her right and handed the ball off to the Hawks' best player, Aja Wheeler. Wheeler was only 5'7" but stronger and faster than anyone else on the court. She had been the person the Hawks counted on at crunch time for years. In what could prove to be the final game of her final season, Cooper would count on her to deliver once again. Wheeler took a moment to examine the defense. Fifteen seconds now stood between the Wildcats and the section championship trophy. Then the Cooper star began her attack.

Wheeler drove hard down the left side of the free-throw lane, but the Wildcats defense formed a wall and wouldn't allow her into the paint the way she had planned. Having successfully diverted Wheeler further from the hoop, when the Cooper star picked up her dribble, she found herself forced to throw up a shot from the left baseline, moving at full speed, from about 10 feet away from the basket. When she let go of the ball, Wheeler went flying out of bounds—not because she was pushed by a Wildcats defender but because she had accelerated at the basket with such speed and power that the sheer force of her momentum propelled her beyond the end line.

The ball floated toward the backboard while Wheeler hit the hardwood. It bounced off the glass and, in defiance of the laws of physics, somehow careened through the rim. Cooper had catapulted back into the lead with just 12 seconds left.

Though the Wildcats had timeouts remaining, they had been coached not to use one in this situation. The strategy was to get the ball inbounds as quickly as possible after the opponent scored and to advance it up the floor for a shot. There were several perceived advantages to this approach, according to their coach. First, the Cats may be able to catch the other team celebrating rather than retreating on defense, perhaps creating a five-on-four or five-on-three advantage. Second, in the scramble and emotion of the final seconds, the opponents may forget whom they were guarding. Attacking a broken defense could create an advantage. Taking a timeout would allow the opposing team to emerge from their bench more composed. A timeout would also offer the Hawks an opportunity to make sure they were each assigned a player to guard as they walked onto the floor and prepared for the ball to be passed in.

The Wildcats had practiced this scenario on several occasions. They knew what to do, so the moment the ball exited the net, a Wildcat was there to retrieve it. Raptor quickly stepped out of bounds, and as she had been coached to do, she immediately fired the ball back in. However, Cooper had neither celebrated nor retreated on defense. After the made basket, the defending champs immediately sprung into a full-court press, something rarely done in that situation. Not anticipating such a move by the Hawks, the quick pass thrown in by the Wildcats landed right in the hands of a Hawks defender. Waconia was forced to foul. With 10 seconds left, Cooper would step to the free-throw line with a chance to expand on a 51–50 lead.

Again the Waconia faithful screamed as loud as their lungs would let them, hoping the sound waves they created could push the crucial Cooper free-throw attempt off the mark. Whether it was nerves or the noise, Cooper missed the first free throw of the bonus and the Wildcats corralled the rebound. However, Cooper had still been whistled for only four fouls. This meant they had "fouls to give." The shrewd strategic move would be to foul Waconia on purpose, forcing the Wildcats to pass in from the side and reset their offensive attack. If Cooper could successfully foul once or twice, it would erase a few more fleeting seconds from the clock.

As they should have, the moment the Wildcats caught the inbounds pass, the Hawks fouled immediately. Waconia would get the ball on the sideline with eight seconds left. Once again the Wildcats caught the pass and Cooper clubbed them, using their sixth foul in short order. Four and a half seconds were left on the clock. The ball still belonged to Waconia. The Wildcats still trailed by one. But now Cooper couldn't foul the Cats again without surrendering a free throw. It was Waconia's turn to call timeout.

The Wildcats would have one last chance to exorcise the demons that had haunted the program for decades, and perhaps as important, they had the confidence that they would do it. Despite the seemingly dire circumstances, the team and their fans could feel that this time was going to be different.

On the previous pass in, the Cooper defender guarding the ball out of bounds had been jumping up and down while doing it. The Wildcats hadn't practiced it much, but they had a special play to run when a defender guarded the ball in that manner.

Fran, a 6'2" post player and the only senior on the Wildcats' roster, would start at the block by the basket. When the ref handed the ball to be put in play, Fran would run up to the wing to receive the inbounds pass. Post players aren't usually closely defended out near the three-point line, so Fran would have the best chance of catching an uncontested pass.

The dynamic defender who had secured the steal to put the Wildcats back in the lead with a minute remaining—and Waconia's leading scorer—Snake would be the person passing the ball in to Fran. As soon as Snake passed it, she was directed to cut quickly toward the basket. Because she would be jumping up and down, Snake's defender would not be in position to keep up with this quick cut. Fran would pass to the cutting Snake, Snake would make the layup, and the Wildcats would finally win the big game. They were finally going to go to state.

"What if Snake isn't open?" Fran asked before the team left the huddle. "Can I drive?"

"Yes, you can drive it!" her coach hollered. "But Snake will be open."

The crowd had been on its feet during the agonizing and action-packed final minutes, and the fans roared in anticipation again as the Wildcats took the floor. In the course of our daily life, four and a half seconds is a miniscule, meaningless amount of time, but in a basketball game with a one-point margin, four and a half seconds can feel like forever.

The official blew his whistle and handed the ball to Snake. Fran cut up to the wing with her hands high to provide a target to her teammate. Snake passed it to Fran, but this time Snake's defender did not jump. Instead, as Snake made her cut to the basket, the defender was locked on to her. Fran, in an attempt to stick to the plan, took an extra second to get the ball to Snake. Because she was not open on the initial cut, Snake had to dart back out toward the corner to gain some separation from her defender. One of these teams had only two seconds left in its season; the other team would move on to Minneapolis.

For years the Wildcats bench had been coached to count down the time if their team had the ball with 10 seconds or fewer left, but in the excitement of the moment, no one was counting. With the noise of the crowd consuming the gym, it's unlikely Snake could have heard the countdown anyway. With the internal clock in her head nearing zero, Snake lofted a last-second shot from nearly the same spot on the baseline where the Cooper star had made her shot to propel the Hawks into their narrow lead moments before.

As the buzzer sounded and the light surrounding the exterior of the glass backboard burned red, the ball bounced off the front of the rim, flew up nearly a foot above the cylinder, then plunged to the floor without going in. Fran and Snake collapsed on the court to join it. In an instant the two Wildcats, the rest of their team, and really the rest of the town went from confidence and hope to despair and devastation.

The contrast between the two teams was obvious once more. As Cooper and their fans embraced and celebrated on one end of the court, the Wildcats were crushed and crying at the other end.

This time was supposed to be different.

CHAPTER 2

Always the Bridesmaid

It would not be accurate to say the Waconia girls basketball program had suffered for 100 years, but it had been pretty close. In the early 1900s, high school girls basketball was thriving in rural communities throughout Minnesota; by some estimates, as many as 350 towns fielded teams. The game was certainly different then from the way it is played today. Rules were modified to accommodate the perceived "frailty" of females. While the boys wore uniforms largely similar to those seen today, the early girls teams wore thick wool uniforms with comparatively little skin exposed. The wool uniforms weren't worn merely to promote modesty; they proved practical as well. In an era when many boys basketball teams enjoyed the comforts of a school gymnasium with bleachers to accommodate crowds, the girls were often relegated to playing in cold barns in the dead of winter. Such was the case for the first Waconia girls basketball team. Formed before cars were common, the team traveled by train to neighboring towns.

As early as 1913, Minnesota boys were able to end their season with a tournament crowning a state champion. There were no such celebrations for the girls. The girls were not considered to be "competing" but rather engaging in mere recreation. Of course, that is rarely how the girls perceived it.

In the late 1930s, with the number of girls teams already on the decline, the Minnesota Department of Education issued an edict that any high school continuing to offer girls basketball should disband its program. By the time the United States entered World War II, Minnesota high school girls basketball appeared to be a thing of the past.

Without basketball for three decades, a full generation of girls grew up without an opportunity to prove their athletic skill and ability on the court. Then a landmark piece of legislation was passed in 1972, the most prominent provision being what is famously referred to as Title IX. The law states that "no person in the United States shall, on the basis of sex, be excluded from participation in, be denied the benefits of, or be subjected to discrimination under any education program or activity receiving Federal financial assistance." Because the crucial word *activity* was included in the language, girls high school basketball was reborn, not just in Minnesota but nationwide.

In the far less politically correct 20th century, Waconia High School's team name was the Chiefs. The reincarnation of the Waconia Chiefs girls basketball team played its first varsity season in 1973–74. That season also marked the beginning of a long and horrible history of heartbreak.

From that first season of the "modern era" through 1997, Minnesota divided high schools into two classes for basketball. Class AA was home to the 128 largest schools, many of them in the Twin Cities metro area. Class A was largely the domain of rural Minnesota towns, and Class A was where Waconia would reside. With more than 300 teams playing Class A ball, the road to the Class A State Tournament was a difficult one. It is for that reason that only three Waconia teams reached the precipice of the ultimate prize: a regional championship trophy and a trip to Minneapolis.

The 1978–79 team was the first to fall one win shy of the state tournament. They finished the season 19–4 and were champions of district 17A. A win in the region semifinal sent Waconia to the Region 5A championship game, where they lost to Albany. The Chiefs returned to the region final five years later, where they were forced to settle for runner-up once more.

The 1988–89 Chiefs were, without a doubt, the best Waconia girls basketball team of the two-class era. Led by dynamic young head coach Mark Pudlitzke, the girls got the town's attention by incorporating a flashy pregame warm-up routine complete with balls spinning on fingers and the Harlem Globetrotters' trademark song "Sweet Georgia Brown" blaring over the gym's tin speakers.

The entertaining show was not limited to warm-ups. The Chiefs rolled to an 18-win regular season, including an astonishing 100–10 trouncing of rival Rockford. The stellar regular season earned the Chiefs the No. 1 seed in the district tournament. After vanquishing their first four foes, Waconia was again one win from the Class A state tournament. The only thing that stood in their way was the Eagles of Eden Valley–Watkins. Separated by 67 miles, the teams would play for the prize in front of a packed house at St. Cloud State University.

Waconia narrowly won the first quarter but trailed by nine at halftime. The Chiefs had punished opponents with a ferocious full-court press during the regular season. With only 16 minutes remaining in the region championship, they relied on their trademark press to get them back in the game. The defensive adjustment worked. With three minutes on the clock, Waconia had trimmed the lead to two. The momentum was squarely with the Chiefs. The only thing that could slow Waconia down was a whistle. In the span of a few seconds, Waconia's two best players were called for their fifth fouls, disqualifying them from competing in the closing moments. With the momentum and their star players stolen away, Waconia came up short once again, falling 66–59.

When Minnesota made the move to a four-class system in 1997, Class AAAA was reserved for the 64 schools with the largest ninth- through twelfth-grade enrollment. Class AAA consisted of the next-largest group of 64 schools. Class AA had 128 teams, and Class A featured another 150-plus programs.

While the high school league was making major changes to the class structure, a separate movement had signaled the end of an era for many high school mascots. Several schools across the Midwest had mascots associated with Native American culture. As local tribes expressed their offense, Waconia joined the wave of Minnesota schools that transitioned away from their traditional mascot in 1994. The newly named Waconia Wildcats were still small enough to compete in Class AA. However, given the town's rapid growth in the early 2000s, Waconia quickly climbed into Class AAA.

It was a flurry of devastating finishes in the 2000s and 2010s that secured Waconia's reputation as the best program in Minnesota never to make a state tournament. Just two wins away from state in 2004–05, the Wildcats took on Minneapolis North. The Cats were up by two with 30 seconds left when a sudden steal by North led to a layup that tied the game. Moments later another Waconia turnover gave North the ball back and the Polars scored with just three seconds left to earn a 40–38 victory. Minneapolis North won their next game by a comfortable margin and coasted past all three opponents at the state tournament to claim the AAA crown.

The following year Waconia won 21 games before battling private-school powerhouse Benilde–St. Margaret's in the section championship, the final win needed to get to state. The Wildcats had lost to the Red Knights 67–54 in a regular-season matchup just three weeks prior, but Waconia had learned from the loss and was well prepared for the rematch. It was a back-and-forth contest with neither team having a lead larger than four points at any juncture. In the closing minutes, some questionable calls by the officials allowed Benilde to beat the Wildcats by four. In fact, the calls were so controversial that the Waconia head coach received an unprecedented apology from the officials after the game. Of course, the apology did nothing to alter the outcome. As was the case the year before, the team that triumphed over the Wildcats toppled all three competitors at the state tournament by double-digit margins on their way to the state championship. It was a championship Waconia players and fans couldn't help but feel could have been— or more likely should have been—theirs.

The 2008–09 team had another 21-win season that featured only six losses. They collided with conference rival Orono for the right to advance to state. The score was tied at 40 with 10 seconds to play. The ball belonged to Orono. Because the Cats had been called for so many fouls in the second half, the Spartans were in the "double bonus," meaning Orono would get two free throws if Waconia were to foul them again. With the fear of being called for another foul firmly embedded in their minds, the Waconia players were defending rather delicately. In their reluctance to get flagged with another foul, the timid Wildcats allowed an Orono player to walk in for a layup at the buzzer. Another outstanding season ended painfully close to the promised land.

Waconia rebounded the following season to win 22 games, a total that tied the record set by the 1989 team for most wins in a season. While the Wildcats were consistently considered among the best in their class, basketball fans around Minnesota were convinced there was something special about this particular version of the Wildcats. They spent the season ranked among the top five teams in the state, and they were the No. 1 seed in their section tournament.

After lying dormant for a few years, an old Waconia nemesis had rebuilt and was on the rise. In the new era of "open enrollment"—a state law allowing students to enroll at schools beyond the borders of where they lived—the Minneapolis North Polars had become the favorite team for the top players in Minneapolis to congregate. Some coaches accused the Polars of recruiting, but however it happened, North had assembled some of the best young players in the city. The Polars roster was populated primarily by eighth and ninth graders; despite their youth, North put together a nice 16-win season. But 16 wins were only good enough to earn the fourth seed in the Wildcats' always-strong section. North and Waconia both took care of business in the early rounds of the playoffs, setting up a showdown in the section semifinals. A recent change to the way section tournaments were administered meant that as the top seed, Waconia would gain the advantage of playing on their home court until the section championship game.

At the time, Waconia High School's gym could hold around 2,000 fans. Somehow the gym must have "magically" grown to fit 5,000 fans for the big game, because at least that many residents claim they witnessed the stunning turn of events that unfolded in the final minutes of the contest.

The Cats were in command, leading by four with two minutes to play. North was forced to foul. Wisely the Wildcats made sure to get the ball into the hands of their best free-throw shooter. Their top sniper was fouled three separate times in the closing moments. A better-than-80-percent free-throw shooter during the season, this consistently clutch player twice missed the front end of a one-and-one and missed both free throws on a two-shot foul. Had she made even one of the four tries, history would have turned out differently. Instead with only a few seconds remaining, the Polars had taken advantage of the miscues and pulled to a tie. North was known for their full-court pressure, and they applied it immediately after evening the score. The Cats were undaunted by the Polars' pressure and cut through it with remarkable ease. In fact, Waconia's press break was so successful that one of their players found herself alone for a wide-open layup as time expired. She made the shot and the gym exploded with joy.

But while Wildcats fans and players were jumping and embracing, the referees gathered in discussion. When the officials emerged from their huddle, they had determined the shot had left the Wildcat's hand one-tenth of a second after the buzzer had gone off. Waconia had been in full celebration mode for more than a minute when they were told the game would be going to overtime.

It would be difficult for any group to go from the thrill of what was a last-second win to resuming the focus and intensity required to prevail in an overtime period. With nearly all four of the over-time minutes exhausted, and both teams exhausted as well, the score was tied once again. The ball belonged to North, and they were attempting to get the final shot against the veteran-laden Wildcats defense. With just more than a second remaining, the Polars passed the ball to an eigth grader in the corner, and this time with just one-tenth of a second *remaining*, she released the ball and it splashed through the net. Yet again less than a second separated the Wildcats from a win; once more a fraction of a second rendered the team and their fans devastated.

Coach Tom Doyscher guided the team through the late 1990s and through the torment of the 2000s. When he resigned after the 2010–11 season, he left having accumulated the most wins of any coach in Waconia history. But like those who came before him, Coach Doyscher couldn't quite get the team over the top.

Despite the team being decimated by injuries, the 2011–12 season still held some hope. Waconia had cobbled together 20 wins even though four of the team's top eight players had been lost at different points during the season to ACL injuries. The 20 wins were only enough to get the Wildcats the No. 4 seed in their always-loaded section. Despite holding a four-point lead with four minutes to go at top-seeded Richfield, the annual collapse unfolded and another season ended with Waconia asking, "What might have been?"

The 2013–14 Wildcats were another team that grabbed the attention of basketball fans across the state. Having graduated the last in what had been a remarkable run of 6'2" post players, the Cats roster was now a collection of undersized guards, many of whom were adept three-point shooters. With a lightning-fast point guard by the name of Anna Schmitt to lead them, Waconia implemented a style of play they dubbed Fun and Gun. The Cats played the fastest pace of any team in the state, pressing and trapping constantly. They fired up three-point shots with impunity. Because they played in a conference full of towering post players, the Wildcats knew that if they played a traditional half-court game, they would not be able to match up. That is why they decided to push the pace. In an attempt to negate the impact of the opposing teams' taller players, the Fun and Gun Wildcats won their first game of the season 111–104. They won the next game 91–68 and they never slowed down. The team went on to shatter several state records, including most points per game (94.4), and they even made their way into the national record book in a few categories. Unfortunately all the records and attention did not alter the outcome in the playoffs.

The Fun and Gun Wildcats led by three with less than 10 seconds to play. The opposing team had the ball. Then something happened that, after all the years of bad luck and frustration, Waconia fans should have come to expect. The unlikely finish crushed them nonetheless. A player on the opposing team, one who had not made a three-point shot all season, cast up a prayer from beyond the arc. The ball banked in off the backboard to send the game to an improbable overtime. The Waconia kids could not recover emotionally from this most recent smite by the basketball gods. The game slipped away in overtime and the Cats lost by eight.

The aforementioned Anna Schmitt averaged 29 points per game in that record-setting season and came back to lead Waconia for one more year, her last before graduation. During her senior season, the Wildcats played a modified version of their fast-paced game. Again they led the state in scoring, though it wasn't by the massive margin it had been the season before. Despite the more disciplined approach, Schmitt still scored an eye-popping 27 points per game and propelled the Wildcats to another No. 1 seed in the section tournament. The top seed meant Waconia once again had home-court advantage through the playoffs, meaning the home fans would be forced to witness another shocking, frustrating defeat.

Officiating would again factor prominently in the outcome of this upset. One of the Wildcats' top scorers, a player known for her calm, unflappable demeanor on the court, was whistled for a technical foul in what had already become a very contentious second half. A few minutes later, with the Waconia fans fully in a frenzy over what they perceived as unfair officiating, the Wildcats coach erupted after another questionable call. He whipped off his suit coat and fired it five rows up into the student section. The coach was rightly tagged with a technical foul. Despite these developments, Waconia found themselves down by only four with a few minutes left when the most egregious of the offenses to transpire against them took place.

After a missed shot by the opposing Richfield Spartans, a scrum ensued for the rebound. As a collection of players congregated around the ball, one of the players from Richfield proceeded to punch a Wildcats player in the face. To be clear, this was not a slap. Captured clearly on video, it was a closed-fist wallop to the jaw worthy of a world championship boxing match. When none of the three officials blew their whistle to penalize the punch, it felt like the furious fans of the home team may storm the court. However, the game was still in the balance, so the fans refrained. A few excruciating minutes later, another promising Wildcats season ended in a calamitous six-point loss. When video of the assault circulated on social media, Richfield responded by suspending the offending player for the first five minutes of the section champion-ship, a game the Spartans won easily to earn what would have been Waconia's spot in the state tournament.

By now it should be evident that Waconia's loss to Cooper at the start of our story was not simply a disappointment. It was another awful chapter in what had been a long history of heart-break. When Cooper crushed the Cats' latest attempt to get to state, it marked the conclusion of Waconia's 45th season in the modern era. The program had collected 9 conference champion-ships and won more than 600 games during that span. In the 23 years since Minnesota had moved to the four-class system, only 22 of the 128 teams in the state's two largest classes had failed to make a state tournament. None of those 22 teams had enjoyed the level of sustained success the Waconia Wildcats had.

Folks around Waconia were convinced their Cats were cursed. It was the only way to explain how the team could consistently lose in such strange and soul-shattering ways. If it wasn't a curse, then it had to be a conspiracy.

Minnesota's Class AAA consists of 64 teams divided into eight sections. As you might expect, the state playoff bracket looks very similar to a bracket one might fill out during March Madness. Every two years the Minnesota State High School League reviews school enrollment numbers and shuffles the sections around based on student populations and geography. If Waconia wasn't the victim of a conspiracy, how else could one explain the way several of the top-ranked teams in the state always seemed to find their way into Waconia's section each time the reshuffle happened?

When Minneapolis North was in the midst of their dynasty, they were always in Waconia's section. When North was on the decline, they were finally moved to a different section. The Polars were replaced by private-school powers Benilde–St. Margaret's and DeLaSalle. When DeLaSalle was dropped from the section, the newly christened No. 1 team in the state was magically moved in and blocked the Wildcats' path to the state tournament. During 18 years in Class AAA, a team from Waconia's section won the state championship an astounding nine times. For Waconia fans, that defied coincidence.

In many ways, the Wildcats' history mirrored that of another prominent Minnesota team that sported the same purple and gold Waconia claimed as school colors. The Minnesota Vikings have been one of the most consistently successful franchises in NFL history. However, the Vikings' regular-season success has never translated to the postseason. They have lost in the NFC Championship Game six times. They have come up short in the Super Bowl on four occasions. As the Vikings and their fans have been tormented by all these near-misses, their neighbors across the Mississippi River in Wisconsin have enjoyed several Super Bowl triumphs. While the similarities are strong, in many ways the string of postseason setbacks has been worse for the Wildcats. The Vikings never had to deal with the top team in the NFL being moved into their division every time the Packers floundered.

While the Wildcats wallowed after the crushing loss to Cooper, there was potentially more bad news looming. The biennial reassignment into new sections was about to be announced by the Minnesota State High School League. As Waconia's population continued to grow, so did the likelihood that the Wildcats would be bumped up to the state's biggest class.

Minnesota's largest class of high school basketball is an entirely different animal than any of the classes below it. With 1,200 high school students, Waconia was one of the largest schools in Class AAA. The smallest school in their class had about 600 students. If they were bumped up to AAAA, the Wildcats would immediately be the smallest school of the 64 with an enrollment that was dwarfed by the 3,000-plus students at schools such as Wayzata or Minnetonka. Some of those enormous schools were only 15 or 20 miles from Waconia, and the Wildcats would almost certainly end up in their section.

These large schools' rosters were routinely full of college scholarship talent. Some high school coaches would joke that they were playing the University of Eden Prairie or the U of M (meaning the University of Minnetonka), but it really wasn't that much of an exaggeration. It wasn't merely a "gap" that divided the top teams in AAA from the top teams in AAAA. It was the Grand Canyon. If the MSHSL announced Waconia was moving up to AAAA, it could be another 20 years before the team would have a realistic shot at reaching its first state tournament. Privately Waconia administrators had confided to the coaching staff that the jump was virtually certain to happen. Already dismayed by recent events, the Wildcats coaches were left to wonder if they would ever catch a break.

Just three weeks after the catastrophic loss to Cooper on March 28, the coaches received an answer, and it came in the form of a resounding yes! When the MSHSL released the new classifications, not only had the Wildcats managed to remain in Class AAA by the narrowest of margins (they were a mere six students shy of the cutoff), they also learned that Cooper was being moved back up to AAAA.

There was a rush of relief and optimism from the players and coaches after that initial announcement. This team that came seconds from the state tournament would return every player for the upcoming season except one. While the 6'2" post player affectionately referred to as Fran was important to the team, there were some talented young players ready to replace her. With a reprieve to remain in Class AAA for at least two more years, the Wildcats would certainly begin the season ranked in the top 10 and be one of the favorites not only to get to state but to win the championship.

Of course, all of that was assuming the MSHSL wouldn't engage in the utter cruelty that had become their calling card and move one or more of the other top AAA teams into Waconia's section. After all, the departure of Cooper did leave a hole in the section that would need to be filled. As soon as the Wildcats remembered their tendency to get placed with other powerful teams, their fleeting optimism receded and trepidation returned.

With a full week in between the announcement of the classifications and when the league would unveil the new sections, the

Wildcats coaches were feverishly attempting to anticipate what team might replace Cooper. The staff determined there were four likely scenarios. Three would put the Cats in favorable circumstances where they would be strong favorites to win the section. The fourth possibility would place defending state champion DeLaSalle back in Waconia's section. Based on history, the coaches were quite certain that was the scenario they would see.

Finally the day arrived. Coaches across the state were camped in front of their computers, frantically refreshing the MSHSL website. When the AAA sections materialized on the screen, the Wildcats coaches anxiously examined the list of teams in section six. The teams were always listed in alphabetical order. Benilde–St. Margaret's was listed first. The Cats had vanquished the Red Knights in the semifinals just a few weeks earlier, and Benilde was buoyed by a roster heavy with seniors. Benilde would be rebuilding and would not be a threat. Bloomington Kennedy had moved down from AAAA to join the section. They had taken the spot vacated by Cooper's elevation back to the biggest class. It was a tremendous "trade," as the Eagles had struggled mightily in recent years and would not win the section. Familiar foes Delano, Mound, and Orono were still on the list and the Cats were 20 points better than all of them. In fact, the only name on the list that posed any threat at all was the Academy of Holy Angels. Another private school just south of Minneapolis, their team was not-so-modestly named the Stars. Holy Angels was good, but they certainly didn't pose the challenge Cooper or previous section rivals had.

Then when the coaches reached the bottom of the section six list, they realized Waconia was not on it! What on earth was going on? Section six had been the Wildcats' postseason home for more than a decade. There must have been a typo or an oversight.

Quickly the coaches started to scan the other seven sections until finally they found themselves mysteriously moved into section two. Two was a section consisting of schools scattered throughout the southwest portion of the state. After 10 years in a section of metro and suburban schools, the Wildcats curiously found themselves clustered with opponents from rural areas, some of which were more than 100 miles away.

When they managed to get over the shock of being in an entirely unexpected section and they looked over the list of teams, it started to settle in that the Wildcats had indeed finally caught a break. Yes, there were some good teams in section two, but none would spend any time ranked as the No. 1 team in the state. Perhaps the curse had been lifted. This unexpected development may mean a 45-year history of heartbreak would finally come to a merciful end. It was too early for these eternal bridesmaids to start shopping for a wedding dress, but Waconia was ready to send out save-the-date cards for March 5, the day of the section championship game.

CHAPTER 3

Neibs

While the Wildcats were overwhelmed with grief after Cooper had authored the most recent chapter in their history of heartbreak, perhaps no one associated with the team took the loss harder than junior varsity coach Dusty Neibauer. Players, coaches, and colleagues referred to him by the nickname Neibs (pronounced Ny-bz). He had come to Waconia High School fresh out of college in the fall of 2004. He immediately joined the girls basketball staff as an assistant and had continued in that capacity for 15 years.

With dark hair that flowed to nearly shoulder-length, Neibs was immediately embraced by the community because of his youthful enthusiasm and his love for the game. He stood about 5'10" with a strong jaw that jutted out just slightly in front of the rest of his face. His legs were thick and muscled from his many years of playing basketball for hours on end. Known as a quick, explosive point guard in his youth, Neibs still possessed the ability to race past his peers during early-morning pickup games before school. On Wildcats game days, he was sure to wear his trademark canvas

Converse shoes, often with the laces completely removed. He also frequently found a way to incorporate a splash of his favorite color, orange, into his daily ensemble.

His classroom could have passed for a college dorm room, or more specifically, the dorm room of a guy who didn't have a girlfriend. The walls were adorned with movie posters, including several from the *Avengers* series. There was a life-size replica of R2-D2 positioned just inside the door to greet students as they entered class each day. Like his level of exuberance, his classroom had barely changed since his first day at Waconia High School.

While his youthful attitude had remained intact, other things had evolved during Dusty's decade and a half as a language arts teacher. After several seasons of coaching punctuated by frustration and disappointment, his hair had thinned. Rather than trying to hide it, Neibs trimmed his once flowing locks in a manner more in keeping with what is commonly expected from a man in his mid-30s. A few feathers of grey had found their way into the hair that remained. He may have lost some hair, but Neibs had certainly not lost his love for basketball.

That said, it was clear that the Cooper loss hit him particularly hard. After the game, he was as dejected as any player; for days afterward, he was not himself. The frustration of coming mere seconds away from the state tournament yet again was almost more than he could handle.

Neibs had a front-row seat to 15 seasons of sadness. That means he had been witness to 33 percent of the modern era of Waconia girls basketball history. As he slowly recuperated from the most recent disappointment, a fresh resolve was beginning to grow inside of him. He was adamant that he and the team would not feel this way again. And Neibs knew that there was a high probability he would get the opportunity to finally erase the team's troubled past by directing the Wildcats to the state tournament himself.

Two years prior to the Cooper loss, the Wildcats head coach had indicated to the staff that he would like to resign. His kids were getting older and he was starting to miss out on their games, concerts, and events. He had been trying to convince someone on the Cats' very competent coaching staff to step up and take the reins. Dusty wanted to, but he didn't have the most crucial component: the blessing of his wife. With two young kids of his own, sliding over a seat into the role of head coach would be considerably more time-consuming. Neibs knew it would be challenging for his family. Without his wife's support, it wasn't going to happen.

Then two months before the Cooper game, the head coach made it clear that this season would indeed be his last. He reiterated his hope that someone on the staff would apply for the position. Dusty discussed it with his wife. He highlighted how much he wanted to run his own program and how important it was to him to see the team have continued success. His wife surrendered.

Neibs was one of three candidates to interview for what was widely considered a very attractive coaching job. The Wildcats returned a talented roster from their 21-win season, and the move to section two meant the team had an excellent chance to reach the state tournament. Neibs took nothing for granted. He produced dozens of documents outlining his philosophy and detailing how he would run the program. If the hiring committee read through the entire pile of paper he included with his application, that may be what caused the committee to wait for five agonizing days after the interview before ultimately offering Neibs the job.

From the instant he accepted the position, Dusty was driven. He had no intention of erasing all the awful memories of past seasons. He was determined to use those failures as fuel, as motivation. He was hell-bent on bringing his team to the state tournament, and not just because of the deluge of disappointment that he had experienced while at Waconia.

Dusty grew up in a small town in northwestern Minnesota, Fertile, right on the edge of where the prairie meets the pines. Fertile is a town of 800 people. It is so small that it was forced to combine with Beltrami (population 100) 12 miles away to form a single school that taught kindergarten through 12th grade. When Dusty was in his teens and wanted to take a girl on a date to see a movie, Fertile was so removed from the rest of the world, the pair was forced to drive an hour to the nearest theater—in Grand Forks, North Dakota.

In 1996, when Dusty was in eighth grade, his small-town Fertile-Beltrami Falcons defied the odds and made it all the way to the state championship game. This was during a brief two-year window when the Minnesota State High School League took the top eight teams from Class A and the final eight from Class AA and combined them to create a Sweet 16 tournament. The concept was to crown a single state champion. The Falcons, with a high school enrollment of about 100, squared off with the most dominant of the many Minneapolis high schools, the North Polars. It was a true David vs. Goliath matchup, but unlike the ending in the classic basketball movie *Hoosiers*, David did not prevail. Dusty's dad was the athletic director for the Falcons, so Neibs got to tag along for every moment of that exciting run to the state championship. It made an indelible impression.

By the time Dusty was a senior at Fertile-Beltrami High School, Minnesota had moved to the four-class system the state still uses today. Running four separate state tournaments meant it was easier for an underdog such as the Falcons to qualify for state. Unfortunately, running four separate state tournaments also meant that only the final four in each class could make the trip to the Twin Cities. Dusty's Falcons flew to a fantastic 21–10 record in his final season. A victory in the section championship game granted Neibs the trip to state he had coveted since middle school.

The Class A quarterfinal contest was played at Concordia College in Moorhead, just across the Red River from Fargo, North Dakota. There was a great atmosphere for the game, but it still fell well short of the bedlam and bright lights Neibs had experienced in the Twin Cities when he tagged along with the team as an eighth grader. It was great, but it didn't feel like a true state tournament game. Dusty's Falcons fell in that first-round game. They never made it to Minneapolis.

Dusty had been denied the chance to play at vaunted Williams Arena, home of the University of Minnesota Golden Gophers. He had come painfully close to his goal of getting to the semifinals, the point at which games were broadcast on statewide television.

The fact that Neibs had come up short of realizing his dream as a high school senior had continued to haunt him. Maybe that was why his pain from the Cooper loss was so magnified. Every time Neibs had watched the Wildcats come up short, he was forced to confront the disappointment from his final game at Fertile. As he took on the title of head coach, Dusty had an absolutely burning desire to lead Waconia to its first state tournament, but below the surface Dusty was definitely driven by some unfinished business of his own.

CHAPTER 4

Three-Car Garages

If you were flying from wherever you are in the world to watch the Waconia Wildcats play, you would fly into the Minneapolis–St. Paul International Airport. However, while the plane made its descent, you would quickly conclude you were not landing in either Minneapolis or St. Paul. That is because when you looked out the window moments before your plane made contact with the runway, you would spot the enormous and world-famous Mall of America a stone's throw from the runway.

If the MSP International Airport is actually in Minneapolis, it is only through the creative gerrymandering of city-limit lines. For all intents and purposes, the airport is in Bloomington, several miles south of Minneapolis. Being in Bloomington means you are only a brief 30-minute drive from your destination.

You head west on Interstate 494, from which you get an even better view of the massive mall that features more than 500 stores, 50 restaurants, and a 7-acre indoor amusement park. A few miles further, on the right side of 494, you see the remnants of what, until

2018, was the Minnesota Vikings practice facility. That means you have made it to Eden Prairie. Now a mere 20 miles separate you from the shores of Lake Waconia.

On a map you can draw a straight line west from Bloomington to Waconia, but to continue on that path, you need to exit 494 and merge onto Highway 5. As was the case with the transition from Bloomington to Eden Prairie, the suburbs blend together so seamlessly you would never know you had crossed into the town of Chanhassen unless you saw the sign advertising the city limits. You pass a bevy of big box stores and chain restaurants, then out the driver's-side window, a sprawling, palatial estate grabs your attention. It was the home of music icon and Minneapolis native Prince. When he built Paisley Park in 1987, it was in a relatively remote location, but with the continued growth of the suburbs, his home is now effectively in the middle of Chanhassen, surrounded by stores and heavy traffic. Continuing west, Chanhassen soon gives way to Victoria, the town where the suburbs finally subside.

Victoria's only stoplight impedes your progress momentarily. Now, fewer than 10 minutes stand between you and your first look at Waconia. As you drive past the Dairy Queen on the edge of town and escape Victoria's city limits, you are immediately embraced by nature. The only sights for the next seven miles are soybean fields, cornfields, and sturdy old trees. This beautiful buffer between the bustling suburbs and small-town life is one of the things that makes it such an attractive place to call home.

You gain your first glimpse of Waconia about a mile outside of town. A water tower with a sailboat silhouette against a burnt-orange sun protrudes prominently above the trees. The only other structure tall enough to sneak above the tree line is the steeple of the Trinity Lutheran Church. Waconia is where the rolling hills of the Mississippi River Valley recede into the remarkably flat, fertile farmland that dominates the western portion of Minnesota. When you drive up an incline on the edge of town, it may be the last hill you encounter for a hundred miles.

A stoplight is the first thing to greet you on the eastern edge of Waconia. At the signal, you are confronted with three choices. Turn right, and you are just two blocks away from a breathtaking view of majestic Lake Waconia. The chamber of commerce is quick to point out the lake is the second-largest in the metro area, trailing only nearby Lake Minnetonka. In the morning and again in the early evening, when the sun hits it just right, Lake Waconia appears as a burst of light shimmering beyond the 150-year-old city cemetery.

A few seconds later you can look to your left and see City Square Park. Comprising a full city block, the park features a large gazebo, a perfect playground for young children, the obligatory picnic shelter, and carved monuments to commemorate every kid from Waconia who served his or her country in war. The first monument was placed in the park in 1897 to honor the city's residents who served in the Civil War. City Square Park also acts as your official welcome to Waconia's Main Street. The drive down Main Street only lasts a few blocks, but between the bank, the bars, and the chiropractor building, you get another glimpse of the lake. When you pass the brewery and the fire department, only two blocks of Main

Street remain. The street comes to an abrupt end because it runs right into Bayview Elementary. Bayview sits on a prime piece of real estate that would make a developer drool, and as recently as the 1960s, it was big enough to school every student in town. All the kids from kindergarten through 12th grade were taught under its roof. The football field where the high school varsity played is still there, just on the other side of the playground.

In the late 1960s Southview Elementary was built a few blocks away and Bayview became a middle/high school. That arrangement worked well until the 1990s. That is when residents voted to raise their own taxes and build a brand-new high school on the west end of town. The explosion of growth that Waconia experienced in the late 1990s and the first decade of the 2000s prompted even more construction. A new middle school was built to the west of the still reasonably new high school. That allowed Bayview to be transformed into the town's second elementary school. It is from the parking lot of Bayview Elementary that you get one of the best views of Lake Waconia's historic Coney Island.

Jutting out from the west end of the lake, the 135-acre island was once home to hotels, restaurants, and even a football field where the University of Minnesota had its annual fall preseason practices in the early 1900s. There has never been a road or bridge connecting the island to the city. The only way to reach it is by boat, or by walking past the hundreds of icehouses that cover the frozen lake in winter. By the 1970s the once-popular tourist destination had fallen into disrepair, and Coney Island has been uninhabited ever since. Though there are signs on the island's shore that warn against trespassing and implore visitors of the dangers of the dilapidated and crumbling buildings, it is still a favorite destination for adventurous high school kids seeking a place to engage in sometimes less-than-legal activities.

When you first pulled into town, the stoplight offered you three different paths. If instead of the scenic drive past the lake, you elected to continue straight, you would notice a building standing several stories above all the others. As you approach the tallest building in town, you see the sign directing drivers to the emergency room with one arrow, to the main hospital with another arrow, and to the professional building with a third arrow. Ridgeview Hospital is the single-largest employer in Waconia, and in some ways it has become the heartbeat of the community.

On the other side of the road, just past the Starbucks and the Dollar Tree, you will notice a strip mall anchored by what, until recently, was the only grocery store in town. Mackenthun's Fine Foods has been a huge part of the community for a century. In the early 2000s it moved from its original location just off Main Street to the growing business district along Highway 5. Directly adjacent to Mackenthun's you will see a series of smaller stores and restaurants where Waconia residents can find everything they need. There's a pizza buffet, a Chinese buffet, a Mexican restaurant, and a large liquor store. If you double back a few blocks east on Highway 5, you will find the farm supply store, the place that carries just about everything you need that you can't find at Mackenthun's.

Had you elected to turn left at the stoplight that greeted you upon your arrival, you would have quickly come upon the Target, which helped launch a great deal of development on the south end of town.

If you aren't from the area, people can tell right away. Locals laugh when tourists attempt to pronounce the town's name. Visitors will say "Wah-cone-ee-ah," but to people who have lived there any length of time, it is pronounced "Wih-cone-yah." Named by the Dakota tribe that first settled the area, *Waconia* is a word that means "fountain or spring" in the native language. European immigrants settled the land in the 1850s, and Waconia was officially granted a charter from the state legislature to become a city in 1880. It fit the stereotype of a small midwestern town for the next 100 years.

After a century of stability, Waconia experienced a rapid evolution in the 30 years that Mark Fredrickson served as the high school principal, from 1988 to 2021. Short, bald, and blessed with a razor-sharp wit, Fredrickson once joked that when he arrived in Waconia, the only diversity the town had was two different denominations of Lutheran. During his days at Waconia High School, he saw the number of students swell from a few hundred to well over 1,000. He witnessed a boom of business and residential housing transform the town from a small hamlet anchored to agriculture into a "bedroom community" where people rested their heads and raised their kids in between commutes to their jobs in the Twin Cities.

Some of the demographics of the town shifted dramatically in the three decades Fredrickson ruled the school with benevolence and a soft-spoken style. For one, the community had become more affluent. A staggering 96 percent of WHS seniors advance to some form of postsecondary education. The median income of Waconia residents is $95,000. That means the average resident makes more than 60 percent above the national average. The median home price is nearly $300,000, again significantly above the $225,000 national average.

Legendary college basketball coach Pete Carril famously announced he did not like to recruit kids who grew up in a house with a three-car garage. He claimed kids from that kind of privilege were too pampered. He thought they never had to fight for anything. Carril certainly would not have pursued any players from Waconia, because the town was covered with three-car garages for as far as the eye could see.

While certain college coaches may not have been interested in Waconia High School basketball players, the people of the town certainly were. The boys teams regularly drew crowds in excess of 1,000 fans for their home games, and while the girls never had as strong of a following, the home-court advantage created by the Wildcats fans was still far superior to the atmosphere generated in every opponent's gym.

Like many small towns, Waconia has its own annual fall festival, Nickle Dickle Day. The event started in 1961 as a way to draw people downtown. The official line from the chamber of commerce is that a store decided to sell things for a nickel. The word *dickle* is allegedly a German term meaning to barter or trade. The locals tell a different, more colorful origin story. Their version involves a Main Street bar that sold beers for a nickel until someone finally used the restroom to take a "dickle." No one wanted to be responsible for the price of beer going up, so patrons would engage in all manner of gyrations and gymnastics to avoid "breaking the seal." No matter how the name was arrived at, the third Saturday in September now serves as the signal to area residents that the cool winds of fall are soon to follow.

Nickle Dickle Day has also become a way to highlight the community's passion for basketball. Several blocks of the street just south of Main are blocked off for pedestrians, food vendors, and a classic car show. City Square Park is packed with people selling crafts from tents and corn dogs from trailers. And at the heart of all the hullabaloo, kitty-corner from City Square Park, is St. Joseph's, a Catholic school that teaches kindergarten through eighth grade.

Every September St. Joe's is host to the biggest outdoor three-on-three basketball tournament in the state. There are divisions for both genders and for all ages from elementary school kids all the way up to adults. Portable baskets are brought in to supplement the already existing hoops that hang in what is typically the school's parking lot. At day's end, when vendors are packing up their wares and the sun seems to be sinking into the lake, the basketball still doesn't stop. It merely moves inside St. Joe's for the girls three-point shootout and the boys slam-dunk competition.

The red bleachers on the south side of the gym hold the first 500 fans willing to part ways with five dollars for admission. Those who make it in always feel fortunate. Seating is so limited, hundreds of fans are turned away and denied the chance to see the state's top high school players scorch the nets and dazzle the crowd with gravity-defying dunks. The north side of the gym has folding chairs set up in rows for local dignitaries, statewide media, and family members of the contestants.

Between the three-on-three tournament, the three-point shootout, and the slam-dunk contest, hundreds of basketball players and thousands of people make the journey to Waconia each September to say goodbye to summer. Nickle Dickle Day has become a beacon to basketball fans around the state and a signal that the fall season is about to begin.

CHAPTER 5

Name Game

At practice, during games, or even walking the hallways at school, players on the Wildcats are never referred to by their actual, legal names. The assignment of nicknames was born out of necessity. The 2013 roster featured two players named Anna and another pair that shared the name Sam. Needless to say, a coach couldn't simply holler out "Anna!" during a game and have both players respond to the same instructions. Because the aforementioned Anna Schmitt was such an explosive scorer, she was anointed with the nickname A-Bomb. The other Anna was not the type of player who could put up 30 points in a game, but in an effort to make her feel equally explosive, she was named Nuke.

Thus began the parade of unique nicknames that have become the team's trademark. Ticket, Barb, Worm, Hammer, Ace, Ralph— these are just a few of what has become a long list of unusual but always affectionate monikers assigned to members of the team. Referees commonly come over to the Wildcats bench during a dead ball or a free throw and ask if what they are hearing is right or if what the coaches are calling the players are really the kids' names.

They may have been born of out necessity, but the nicknames quickly transformed into a team tradition, becoming something of a rite of passage. Ninth graders look forward to the day when they are christened with their new basketball names. Sometimes a name is a play on a girl's first or last name, or her initials. For example, a player with the initials A.C. made one of the coaches think of air-conditioning, so her nickname became Chilly. Another player's initials were L.V.S. A Wildcats assistant realized when you said her initials together it sounded like "Elvis," hence her nickname.

While many names arrive through this kind of thoughtful deliberation, more frequently names are hatched in a more spontaneous or organic manner. A prime example can be found in the name of one of the Wildcats' senior captains. Sauce got her name through a simple misunderstanding.

The Cats practice two mornings a week in the summer. In an effort to ease the transition to high school and to make sure they have built some measure of familiarity with the team's offensive and defensive system, seventh and eighth graders are annually invited to participate in the summer practices. As the head coach was pointing out some of the middle school players to the coaching staff, an assistant coach misheard a last name.

"Did you say her last name is Meat?" asked an assistant.

"You mean like meat sauce?" queried Coach Neibauer. Laughter ensued. In that moment, the unsuspecting young post player had become Sauce through no fault of her own.

Players are not asked for permission or approval before they are given a name. If they were, some of the names would certainly have been rejected. The idea of asking for an alternative nickname was never a consideration for Sauce. She was not the type to let herself get caught up in trivial matters. The team's resident genius (she achieved a nearly perfect score on the ACT test), her superior intellect never impeded her socially. Sauce was the player most likely to make the entire team laugh so hard they cried. She was also the teammate most likely to invoke salty language.

Her mother was an OB/GYN who had delivered close to 20 percent of the students roaming the halls of Waconia High School. Sauce's father was a special education teacher who ran the town's Nickle Dickle Day three-on-three tournament every fall. Both parents played basketball in college, but Sauce had not been gifted with great athleticism. That is not to say she was unathletic; however, Sauce was never going to run the fastest or jump the highest on any team she played on. What she lacked in natural ability, she made up for in guile and gumption. Sauce had an intangible quality the Wildcats had historically lacked: toughness.

There was no such election on the team, but if there were, Sauce would have won Most Likely to Throw an Elbow by an enormous margin. While most of the Wildcats were reluctant to retaliate when receiving a cheap shot, Sauce was not only certain to retaliate but was perhaps the only player on the roster who would instigate animosity from an opponent by launching a preemptive attack.

Sauce stood 5'10" with raven black hair. She had an uncanny ability to anticipate missed shots and position herself where the rebound would come off the rim. An adequate scorer in the paint, Sauce worked hard during her first two years of high school to extend her shooting range. Her dad had the keys to the gym at St. Joe's. The two of them had spent countless hours together in that gym—Sauce shooting, her dad rebounding for her.

The hard work had paid off. By the beginning of her junior year, Sauce had developed into an excellent perimeter shooter. In fact, in an era of analytics when coaches emphasize layups and three-point shots, Sauce was the only player on the team who was actively encouraged to take midrange jump shots whenever she was open. The coaching staff declared that she had "midrange magic," and whenever Sauce would swish a 15-foot jumper, the bench would shout out "Abracadabra!" in celebration.

Sauce's off-season efforts translated into success behind the three-point line as well. In the previous year's regular-season finale, with 1.2 seconds left, the score tied, and the conference championship on the line, it was Sauce who caught a pass in the corner and buried a three at the buzzer to clinch the Wildcats' first conference championship in five years. After a big junior year, she was eager for her senior season to begin, expecting to play an integral role for her highly ranked Wildcats.

The most talented player on the team, Salsa was a 5'11" junior guard who had already received scholarship offers from a few Division I schools. With a lanky, lean frame and a confident air, Salsa caught the eye of college coaches the moment she walked into a gym. Her nickname, a derivative of her real name, described her basketball ability better than it did her personality. In the same way her namesake could start off with a smooth flavor before finishing with a hint of fire, Salsa would knock down a long three-pointer with her picture-perfect form, and seconds later she would burn her opponent by going coast to coast for a contested layup. She had excellent instincts on defense and could be counted on to steal at least one opponent's pass per game. Though she was nearly the tallest player on the team, Salsa could dribble the ball through traffic like a magician, making the ball disappear behind her back at the exact moment a defender lunged for it.

Unlike Sauce, neither of Salsa's parents had been basketball players. She was an entirely self-made star. Salsa had logged more hours in the gym refining her skills than any other player in the program. As much as she loved the game, there was also something Salsa loved about the echo of a single basketball bouncing in an otherwise empty gym. These solo workout sessions were a time for her to reflect and get lost in her own thoughts. It could truly be said that when Salsa was alone on a basketball court, she was in her comfort zone.

Off the court, she had a unique sense of humor that could draw puzzled looks from strangers. However, her oddball antics were always endearing to her friends. More than just an exceptional athlete, Salsa was also a strong student. Though she was what most people would consider the "total package," the confidence she exuded on the court was not always evident as she walked the halls of the high school. Sometimes girls blessed with above-average height feel most at home on a basketball court, surrounded by other girls that look like them. Tall women literally stand out in a crowd when many would much rather blend in. Maybe Salsa wrestled with those same feelings of self-consciousness when she walked among the more vertically challenged masses.

As the calendar turned to November and the team was just two weeks away from the start of their season, the hint of self-doubt Salsa seemed to have in the hallways had, for the first time ever, followed her onto the floor. Tryouts were about to begin, and she wasn't sure she was ready.

Ten months earlier, on a Saturday in mid-January, Salsa had torn the meniscus in her knee. It happened early in the game. No one on the bench was even remotely aware she had been injured. Salsa did not run with any kind of a limp or play with any limitations on her way to another solid 12-point, 5-rebound performance. She did not mention her discomfort to the coaches after the game, hoping her knee would feel better after a weekend to recover. When she woke up on Monday morning, the pain was even more pronounced than it had been the day before. She went to the doctor and was devastated by the diagnosis.

Salsa was relieved it was not a torn ACL, but her knee would still require surgery. The timeline for recovery meant the earliest she could hope to be back was for the section playoff semifinals, and that was a best-case scenario. Even for a deep team, losing Salsa for the final five weeks of the season was a tough blow. The team had already experienced a season-ending injury to a different varsity player, and there was no one on the roster who could step in and rival the variety of ways Salsa could affect a game.

Somehow the team held things together while Salsa rehabbed. They went 6–2 in her absence. She followed the orders of her doctors and physical therapists diligently and was cleared to play 36 hours before the section semifinal game. The coaching staff was eager to get their game changer back on the court, especially given the magnitude of the game. However, the coaches also knew they would have to pick their spots with her. Having been sidelined for five weeks, to play her major minutes would have been reckless. Salsa played 16 minutes and contributed nine points in the Wildcats' 68–54 second-round victory.

Waconia had three days to prepare for the section championship game against the defending state champions. Though Salsa had three full practices to prepare, things were different competing against the faster, more physical Cooper Hawks. In the game's opening minutes, it became clear to the coaches that Salsa was not in a position to have the impact she would have typically had if healthy. That was to be expected. She had only four practices under her belt since her surgery. Because she was not herself, Salsa was not on the floor for the final minutes of the last-second loss. Viewing the frustrating finish from the bench had dealt a blow to her self-confidence. Like most great athletes, Salsa did not consider herself limited in any way. Being denied the chance to make a difference during those final moments had been eating at her for months.

Her summer AAU season should have provided a chance for Salsa to get her "groove" back, but shortly after her club season started, it came to an abrupt end. It was another meniscus tear—this time in her other knee. An honorable-mention All-State player as a sophomore, Salsa suddenly found herself wondering if she was ever going to be an impact player again. Would her knees hold up? Or at only 16 years old were her best days already behind her? She was consumed with worry for weeks, anxiously awaiting the first practice of the season.

There were no such doubts in Snake's mind as she spoke about what would be her senior season. The team's leading scorer as a ninth grader, then again in her sophomore and junior seasons, Snake's nickname took a while to materialize. It was the summer before her junior year when she implored the coaching staff that they needed to finally come up with one.

Among her most distinguishing characteristics on the court were her incredibly quick hands. Snake could pick the opposing point guard's pocket in the blink of an eye and slither to the other end for an easy layup. It was her ability to strike quickly on defense that led to her nickname.

Snake had been so dominant in middle school that she was moved up to the ninth-grade team as an eighth grader. The promotion was, in part, so she could be challenged by better competition. The move would also allow the rest of the eighth graders an opportunity to develop into scorers. Throughout middle school, Snake was such a dominant force that her teammates were often reduced to the role of spectators, gawking at her impressive exploits. To be clear, Snake was never a ball hog; she just had a skill level that surpassed her peers' to the point that she could score almost effortlessly. Snake routinely scored 10 points a game by exploiting the other team's ball handlers, turning steals into layups. She would score 10 more with acrobatic drives through the lane. Despite her eye-popping point totals, Snake could not be credibly accused of being a selfish player. She was every bit as likely to zip a perfect no-look pass to a teammate when the defense double-teamed her. In addition to leading the varsity team in scoring, Snake had also dished out more assists than any player on the team during her three varsity seasons.

Behind closed doors, the coaching staff called Snake the "Brett Favre of high school basketball." Like the legendary Packers and Vikings quarterback, Snake would throw an ill-advised pass that made fans pull their hair out and then, moments later, make a play that made jaws drop throughout the gym. As it had been for the coaches who worked with Hall of Famer Favre, the Waconia staff learned that with Snake, they had to take the good with the bad, and Snake always brought more good to the game than bad.

Snake had been blessed with the ability to make the key play in the closing minutes of a close game. She epitomized the term *playmaker*. Snake started her senior season just 32 points shy of 1,000 for her career. If she stayed healthy, she was likely to finish in the top five on the school's all-time scoring list. There was just one thing Snake lacked to cement her legacy as one of the best ever to wear a Wildcats jersey: a trip to the state tournament.

A friend since first grade and a teammate since fifth, Snake's running mate in the backcourt was a bubbly brunette by the name of Bird. Only 5'6", Bird compensated for her lack of height with an athletic build. The consummate point guard, Bird's top priority was always delivering the ball to an open teammate. As a result, opposing teams would sometimes make the mistake of focusing their defense on Waconia's other weapons. When they did, Bird was certainly skilled enough to make them pay. It was evident in the box scores. Bird would have five or six games in a row where she would score only four or five points, then some ill-informed coach would tell their team, "Make No. 2 beat us." Bird would oblige, leading the Wildcats to a win with a 16-point performance.

Another senior captain, Bird was the most charismatic kid on the team. Off the court she always wore a grin that made it appear she was up to something, and she usually was. Sauce may have been the team comedian, but no one on the team laughed more than Bird. Bird was silly. When most of her teammates were getting homework done in the bleachers during the first half of a JV game, Bird would suddenly stand up and start dancing to the music being blared during a timeout. Sometimes she didn't even need music or a reason to get up and be goofy.

Her fun-loving attitude kept the team from getting uptight, but when Bird stepped on the court, she was a ferocious competitor. In the weeks leading up to the section final with Cooper, Bird had been wrapping her knees in ice for hours each day. After every practice she moved more like an 80-year-old than someone on the cusp of 18. She knew her team was shorthanded at the guard spot due to injuries, so Bird battled through the pain. One teammate said, "She's the only person I've ever met who still has a smile on even when she's suffering." After a summer to recover, Bird's knees were feeling better and she was as driven as her fellow seniors to see her final season end at the state tournament.

Though they had graduated one starter, the Wildcats effectively had five starters returning as they prepared for the approaching season. That is because for the five weeks that Salsa was sidelined after surgery, another guard—Rookie—got the chance to start, and she took full advantage of the opportunity.

Rookie was one of the best three-point shooters ever to walk the halls of Waconia High School. Despite being the first player off the bench for most of her sophomore season (before stepping in as a starter in Salsa's absence), Rookie set a new school record for most made three-pointers in a year. The record was particularly impressive considering the volume of threes that were fired up during the Fun and Gun era. Standing 5'7" with bright blonde hair, Rookie was not physically imposing, and like Sauce, she was not abundantly athletic. That said, if the defense made the mistake of leaving her open outside the arc, she would punish them. Rookie poured in threes with a frequency and ease that resembled the effortless manner in which other players made layups.

During her record-breaking sophomore season, Rookie had been diagnosed with a congenital knee problem. At random times and for seemingly no reason at all, her kneecap would slide out of place. It happened more often while playing, but her malady was not confined to the basketball court. Her kneecap had even dislodged once while merely walking through the crowded halls in between classes.

It was very painful and obviously problematic when playing a game that could be hard on even the healthiest knees. After the diagnosis, she wore braces on both her knees, and like Bird, Rookie was also well acquainted with the team trainer and the ice machine. Outsiders would never know the chronic discomfort she dealt with because beyond being the team's best shooter, Rookie also led the squad in "smiles per day." There was not a more positive person in the program. Rookie was an easy kid for everyone to root for. Though she had been relegated to a reserve role for the first 70 percent of her sophomore season, Rookie was voted first-team All-Conference by opposing coaches. The news inspired no jealousy among her teammates. Everyone was genuinely happy for her. It is impossible to be mad at a person who exudes nothing but positivity.

Even before tryouts began, the starting five seemed set. The top substitutes who would spell the starters seemed almost as clear. After playing major minutes as freshmen, 10th graders Scrunchie and Raptor were certainly going to be key factors for the team.

An affinity for the 1980s and '90s ponytail holder earned Scrunchie her nickname. With dark hair, dark skin, and big brown eyes, she had a wingspan that belied her height. A look at her outstretched arms would suggest she was at least 6'3", but Scrunchie was actually 5'11". Her long arms combined with an excellent leaping ability allowed her to play bigger than she actually was. In terms of her physique, it had transformed significantly over the off-season. A string-bean freshman who sometimes got pushed around by opposing posts, Scrunchie had worked hard in the weight room. She was prepared and determined to do some pushing and shoving of her own when her sophomore season started.

Scrunchie was a remarkably efficient scorer who rarely missed when she attempted a shot in the paint. In addition to taking up residence in the weight room, she had also spent the summer enhancing her skills. Coach Neibauer was excited about her ability to pull other, less athletic posts out of the paint and drive past them. If her defender backed off, Scrunchie had the added advantage of being a legitimate three-point shooter. She was going to be a tough matchup for opposing teams and a real weapon for Neibs to bring off the bench.

The second sophomore the Cats would rely on in a reserve role was Raptor, the strongest and most athletic player on the team. Her brother had been a star baseball player and the starting quarterback at Waconia, and even with that résumé, he was rapidly becoming known as the second-best athlete in the family. Raptor was so explosive she played like she was on a pogo stick.

When arriving at her nickname, the coaches were trying to conjure a creature that was as fast and ferocious as her. The velociraptors from *Jurassic World* were the only predators that could compare. But Velociraptor violated one of the key rules of Wildcats basketball nicknames: it had too many syllables. Ideally nicknames will be one syllable, but they are never allowed to exceed two. They have to be something a coach can yell loudly and quickly. So the two-syllable Raptor would have to suffice.

Raptor was the player who made the layup to give the Cats the lead in the closing minute of the Cooper game. As a freshman, she had already demonstrated an ability to affect the game, and she was doing it largely based on raw athleticism. Only one person on the team could approach her leaping ability, and absolutely no one could keep up with her speed from one end of the court to the other. At 5'8" she was undersized for a post and she did not have the typical ball-handling or shooting skills that guards traditionally possess. Neibs wasn't quite sure where she would fit in as the season approached, but her ability to defend all five positions and her uncommon athleticism meant she would get plenty of playing time.

Another player Neibs knew he would be counting on in a big way was Ozzie. Her name came from the sound her initials—A.Z.—made when you put them together. Ozzie was a lightning-quick point guard who also earned varsity minutes as a freshman. Tragically she had lost nearly all of her sophomore season to a torn ACL (after losing the summer before her sophomore season to a knee injury). In the first six games of that season, when she was healthy, Ozzie was really turning heads. She was so quick and nimble that she could get into the lane for layups seemingly at will.

Even after his resignation, the former head coach continued to lament Ozzie's absence from the team for the balance of his final season. He insisted the Cats would have won at least two more regular-season games and the section championship over Cooper had Ozzie been healthy. Even though her rehab lasted through the summer, Neibs was confident she would be ready to contribute in a big way. Ozzie was not nearly as convinced. As the season approached, she confided in her teammates that she didn't feel quite the same. She lacked confidence that she would return with the kind of quickness that had been such a key element to her game. Ozzie's angst was understandable.

Cars that go 0 to 60 in a few seconds are certainly fun to drive, but they can also be more prone to breakdowns. Ozzie had always been able to accelerate faster than most, but with the season about to get underway, she was leery of putting the proverbial "pedal to the metal." She would have to overcome her fears before she could ever go full-throttle.

If Ozzie faltered or failed to regain her form, there was another talented guard who would swoop in and take on the role of backup to Bird—that is, if she decided to try out for the team. "Mellow Yellow" was her full nickname, but for practical purposes the coaches shortened her moniker to Mel. During elementary and middle school, Mel had played on some elite AAU basketball teams. The previous head coach never seemed impressed by her AAU experience and he claimed to have heard too many stories about her "attitude." As a result, though she was certainly talented, Mel had been relegated to the JV team while most of her fellow sophomores had ascended to important roles on the varsity. Other than a few minutes here and there in "mop-up time," Mel rarely saw the varsity floor. Disillusioned by this, she was openly debating with her family and her teammates about whether she would even bother to try out for the team as a junior.

"The team doesn't need me" was her most common refrain when asked if she was excited for the start of the basketball season. Mel was hopeful her teammates would reach out and encourage her to play. She wanted validation. She wanted to feel needed. Mel made it known she was contemplating trying out for the girls hockey team. An accomplished soccer player, Mel was a gifted enough athlete that she probably could have pulled off the transition to what some have called "soccer on ice," but to most of her teammates Mel's threats rang hollow. They knew her well enough to understand what she was after and most did not give it to her. Instead of pleading for Mel to play, several of her teammates ignored her overtures. A few players even admitted they might be better off without her, not because she lacked ability, but because in their words she was "not a good teammate."

It may have been that Mel was simply misunderstood, a victim of the double standard that has afflicted female athletes since the 1970s and the so-called rebirth of women's team sports. When a male athlete is intense and emotional he is frequently hailed as a "ferocious competitor," but when a female athlete portrays the same characteristics she is often described as "moody," "mean," or worse (say, an unflattering word that rhymes with "itch").

No one disputed that Mel could be intense on the court or that her language toward teammates was often abrasive. Mel didn't play sports to make friends; she played to win.

As a sophomore, Mel had been the leading scorer on the JV team. That team had been coached by new varsity head coach Dusty Neibauer. Neibs knew Mel brought some baggage with her, but he convinced himself he could help reform her sometimes negative nature. He was also of the opinion that Mel could help the team get to the state tournament.

Another of Neibs's JV players whom he expected to play a role on varsity was an undersized but physically strong post player he called Dozer. The nickname was short for her more formal nickname of Bulldozer, bestowed because of her ability to push much bigger players off the block when defending around the rim.

Every class has a kid who developed early and is taller and more dominant than everyone else in seventh grade. That was Dozer. She reached her fully grown height of 5'8" early in middle school. That altitude was impressive for a post player in seventh grade, but it was well below average at the high school level. Dozer was a good player. She just had a tall order (literally) in guarding and in being guarded by opponents who were a half a foot taller. Despite the height difference, she continued to hold her own defensively, though it had become rather difficult for her to get a shot off consistently against bigger posts.

Again, Neibs knew Dozer and what she was capable of. He also knew the team's history with injuries and that she would likely be called upon at various points throughout the season to help the varsity at key moments. The attitude concerns that loomed with Mel would never be a concern when it came to Dozer. She always kept a low profile, never brought drama, and was universally considered to be a good teammate.

Speaking of good teammates, that leads us to the eleventh and final player on the varsity roster. Will was the sometimes-forgotten fourth senior. Forgotten because she had been a JV player as a junior and had been told by Coach Neibauer that if she tried out for the team as a senior she would almost certainly continue in that capacity. As difficult as it was for Will to hear, she loved basketball and would never abandon the game or the teammates she had grown so close to.

Will was not a bad player. In fact, like several of the other kids coming off the Waconia bench, Will could have been a starter for some of the other teams in the conference. Being the worst player on a great team doesn't always equate to being "bad." Will was a good shooter, and there was positively no one in the program as adept at taking charges. Her willingness to get run over in an effort to help her Wildcats win demonstrated what a top-notch teammate Will was. While her heart hurt knowing she would not get the opportunity on varsity she had worked for, an opportunity she thought she had earned, Will never demonstrated even a hint of disappointment around her teammates. As she had done the season before, Will enthusiastically waved a towel at the end of the bench when one of her teammates made a big shot. She continued to be one of the hardest workers at practice because she knew it was the best way to help the team get ready for the next game. On the scout team, Will always played the role of the other team's top shooter, and because she had to learn the opponent's plays to run against the varsity in practice, she could often be heard hollering out the plays from the bench during the game in an attempt to help her teammates know what was coming. She was the undisputed best teammate, and Neibs named her the team's fourth captain for that reason.

Slinger, Cee Cee, Sizzle, Jo-Jo, Slick, and Poe were junior varsity players who were also in uniform for the varsity games, but their real role was to act as the "hype squad." Especially during road games, when the crowds could be sparse and the gym eerily quiet, the JV players would do their best to make it feel like a Wildcats home game by waving towels, shouting encouragement, and even through some fun, choreographed celebrations. Every player had a role as the season began. The issue that hovered over the team and that kept Coach Neibauer up at night was whether each player would accept her assigned role.

CHAPTER 6

The Gauntlet

Given a choice between coaching a roster deep with college-caliber players or leading a team limited in numbers and talent, any sane coach would opt for the team with talent. However, leading a talented team is rarely as simple as it may seem to outside observers. An abundance of talent can certainly present challenges of its own. Veteran coaches will frequently confirm that some of their most difficult seasons (in terms of off-court issues) came when they had their most talented teams.

Coach Neibauer was about to embark on his rookie season as a head coach, but he was not oblivious to the land mines that lay ahead. When Neibs was asked what his biggest challenges were heading into the season, like a veteran head coach, he responded "Managing egos and expectations." The Wildcats were not lacking in either category as the calendar turned to November and the beginning of practice.

With nearly their full varsity rotation returning from a 21-win season, the expectation that the approaching season would be even better than the last extended well beyond Waconia's city limits. Prominent basketball websites and preseason publications were unanimous that the Wildcats were the favorite to win their new section and reach the Class AAA state tournament. No preseason poll had the Cats ranked lower than eighth in the state. One poll put them as high as number three. Neibs knew it would be hard to live up to all the hype. However, he was equally certain his players had the ability to match and surpass the preseason prognostications. Neibs embraced the expectations. He was less confident about his ability to navigate the egos.

The Wildcats had at least 11 players who could rightfully claim to have varsity-caliber ability. Seven or eight players monopolize most of the playing time on a traditional basketball team. It is common to see the starting five get the majority of the minutes and an additional two or three players rotate in off the bench to spell a starter who is in foul trouble or who needs a rest. If Dusty followed a traditional rotation, he would likely have three or four talented but upset players on his team at all times. Of course, if Dusty went deeper into his bench and played all 10 or 11 who merited it, that would mean fewer minutes for his starters, and it is likely some of them would become disgruntled. In the end, having too many talented players is a good problem to have, but it still presents a problem.

Neibs had one other considerable challenge confronting him as the season started. Having anticipated the team making the jump to Class AAAA, Dusty's athletic director had built a remarkably daunting nonconference schedule. Still a Class AAA team, Waconia would open their season with seven consecutive games against AAAA schools. Four of the first seven foes were ranked in the top 10 in the state's largest class. The first five of those seven games were away from the friendly confines of the Wildcats' home court. If the casinos in Las Vegas produced point spreads for high school basketball games, Waconia would have been favored to win only one of their first seven contests to start the season.

Neibs needed to mentally prepare his players (and their parents) for the gauntlet of games they were about to face. At the preseason parent meeting, Dusty explained that to get stronger, players had to lift heavy weights: "You can walk in the weight room, pick up the five-pound weights, lift those the entire time, and walk out feeling like you're pretty strong. The five-pound weights make you feel good about yourself, but they don't make you stronger. When we lift the heavy weights, they may make us feel sore the next day, but that is a sign our muscles are getting stronger. This first month of the season, we are playing heavyweights. We may feel sore after some of these games, but they are going to make us stronger and put us in a better position to get to our ultimate goal: the state tournament."

While Neibs actually believed everything he said to the parents and players, as a new head coach he also would have preferred to mix a few "five-pound weights" into the early season schedule to get his head coaching career off to more of a positive start. His spin about the daunting schedule would only work for a while. With the preseason rankings and the lofty expectations, eventually the

Wildcats would have to win some games or Neibs knew things would get ugly.

Waconia's season began at what was widely considered to be the most prestigious event in Minnesota basketball with the obvious and notable exception of the state tournament. The state's biggest basketball publication, the *Breakdown*, annually hosted a slate of games on the opening Saturday of the season. They called it the Tip Off Classic, and it was an invitation-only event. When a coach got the call asking if his or her team would like to participate, it was truly one of the greatest honors a team could receive. There were 20 games and 40 teams, and nearly every team ranked in the top 10 in each of Minnesota's four classes was there. All of the games were played at one site, Hopkins High School, about 10 miles west of Minneapolis. Hopkins was one of the few schools in the state with the ability to accommodate two varsity games with large crowds being played simultaneously.

Part of the event's appeal was that the *Breakdown* deliberately paired teams from different regions of the state, teams that would not normally play each other. The Wildcats would face Rosemount, ranked No. 8 in Class AAAA. Neibs had never seen the Irish play, so he contacted coaches and asked for video of games from the prior season. Based on what he watched, Neibs anticipated Rosemount would play at a slower pace and sit in a 2-3 zone on defense. The other thing that was evident, even while watching on his computer monitor, was that the Irish were tall. Those were the big bullet points from the first scouting report Neibs typed out for his team.

As the two teams walked out to center court for the jump ball, it became clear the word *tall* in his scouting report should have been in all capital letters, bold font, and underlined. Salsa was the tallest starter for the Cats and she was 5'11". When she stepped into the center jump circle, Salsa was engulfed by the shadow of three players well above six feet in stature.

Despite the height disparity, Waconia won the opening tip, only to turn the ball over a mere 10 seconds later. Rather than walking the stolen ball up as Dusty had seen on video, Rosemount raced up the court and scored a quick layup to take the lead. On the ensuing possession, another Wildcats turnover led to an identical result.

Two minutes into the promising new season, the Rosemount lead had grown to 11–0, and the Irish never looked back. Minnesota high school teams play two 18-minute halves rather than the four eight-minute quarters that are more common around the country. After 18 minutes of action, Waconia was losing 49–28. At halftime the mood in the locker room was subdued but not necessarily discouraged. The players knew they were underdogs going into the game. They had simply hoped the contest would be more competitive. The second half played out much like the first. Rosemount finished the game making a school-record 16 three-pointers and Waconia fell 83–57.

The team Neibs had seen on video looked dramatically different from the group that had just dismantled his squad in the season opener. When asked about it after the game, Neibs said with the slightest hint of a smile, "No one told me that last year they lost their best player to injury for most of the season. They are definitely a different team with her back in the lineup." It was a reminder that for all his accumulated wisdom after many years as an assistant, Neibs was still a rookie head coach.

Again, the Tip Off Classic was played on a Saturday, and the Minnesota State High School League prohibited teams from practicing on Sundays. That meant Waconia had exactly one practice—Monday—to improve on things before they made the 25-mile drive back to Hopkins on Tuesday to face the defending AAAA state champions, the No. 1–ranked Royals.

Hopkins was more than good; they were a powerhouse. Hopkins had not lost a game in 616 days. They were perennially ranked as one of the best high school teams in the country, and they had started this season as the fourth-best team in the nation according to ESPN. *USA Today* had the Royals ranked third in their poll.

How was it that Hopkins could field such formidable teams year after year? Certainly they had good coaching and great facilities, but they had also become the hub where most of the premier players in Minnesota chose to matriculate. The top players on the Royals roster were rarely products of the Hopkins youth program. There was a long-standing joke with Minnesota high school fans that when Hopkins played on the road, the pregame lineups should announce what town the Royals' starters hailed from: "Starting at guard, a 6'2" sophomore from Eden Prairie…"

The other reason Hopkins garnered so much hype from national media outlets was because of their point guard Paige Bueckers. She was the consensus No. 1 high school girls basketball player in the country. Already committed to play for legendary coach Geno Auriemma at UConn, Bueckers was the first female basketball player ever featured on the cover of *Slam* magazine, the country's premier basketball publication. By the time you read this, it is likely Bueckers will already have risen to national prominence with UConn, or after being the top pick in the draft, she is probably dominating the WNBA. Bueckers already had a shelf decorated with gold medals from leading the junior US Olympic team in international competition, and the high school senior was a lock to add a few more gold medals to her collection before her career was complete.

Every bit of six feet tall, with long, blonde hair that was always pulled back into a tight ponytail on the basketball court, Bueckers's frame and her game had conjured comparisons to WNBA legend and former UConn star Diana Taurasi. Both players were strong, fast, and uncommonly coordinated for their height. Both were great shooters and prolific scorers. But the remarkable thing about Bueckers was how her transcendent talent was not limited to shooting or scoring. She also had the ability to control the game as a point guard, adept at creating easy scoring opportunities for her teammates when she wasn't scoring herself. Nicknamed by some opponents the Hopkins Highlight Reel, Bueckers was also able to take over a game on the defensive end with her long arms and remarkable instincts. There were just no weaknesses in her game.

Most of the Wildcats players were excited for the chance to compete against the nation's No. 1 player. They had seen Bueckers featured several times in *Sports Illustrated* and splashed all over social media. "Someday I'll be able to point to her on TV and say, 'I guarded her in high school,'" beamed an exuberant Salsa.

Coach Neibauer's scouting report acknowledged Bueckers's ability: "She tends to want to distribute more than dominate the game with her scoring. If the game is on the line, it will be her taking the shot, but until that time we aren't going to run two at her [double-team her]. If we do that, she will take us apart with her passing. We will deny her when she doesn't have the ball. Anticipate her pulling up for a jumper when she drives. Salsa will start on her."

As the only player on the Cats drawing Division I interest, Salsa was the obvious person to put on a player of Bueckers's prowess. However, Neibs knew it would take more than one player to slow down the UConn recruit. It would take a true team effort.

In the locker room before the game, Neibs again reminded the team of Buecker's strengths and tendencies. He also attempted to instill some confidence in his kids. "Don't double her when she drives or she will dump it off. Yes, she's the No. 1 player in the country, but we don't back down from anyone! We don't fear anyone!" With that, the Wildcats charged out to take on the top team in the state.

If Waconia had needed to worry only about Paige Bueckers, that would have been daunting but manageable. The trouble was Hopkins had at least four other surefire high-level Division I players on their roster. Even if the Wildcats were somehow able to contain the most coveted recruit in the country, there were other top-flight talents ready to carry the Royals.

An excellent crowd had convened for what would be both teams' second game of the season. The bleachers under Hopkins's first-half basket were where Waconia's student section filed in. The Wildcats would be trying to score with a hundred Hopkins students howling a few feet beyond their hoop.

The Royals won possession on the jump, and like steel drawn to a magnet, the ball instantly found its way to Bueckers. She attacked the middle of the lane. As she pulled up for the jump shot Neibs had forecasted in the scouting report, Bueckers was hacked hard from behind by Salsa. Only two seconds had ticked off the clock and Bueckers was toeing the line for two free throws. However, Salsa had sent an early message that she and the Wildcats were not about to bow down to the Royals.

Bueckers swished both free throws and Hopkins launched into their famous full-court press. Waconia knew what was coming, and they were prepared with a press break. The Cats successfully made it past the full-court pressure but threw a panic-stricken pass as they initiated their half-court offense. Hopkins happily intercepted the ball and attacked in the other direction. Bueckers again found herself with the rock and dribbled it toward the middle of the floor. She stopped a step inside the arc to shoot another of her patented pull-up jump shots. Snake got a hand up in the star's face and forced her to miss. The rebound banged hard off the back of the rim, ricocheting to nearly the same spot it had been shot from. Snake was there to corral it. She then raced up the court and found Sauce open in the lane. Snake zipped a perfect pass to her fellow senior. Sauce had her back to the basket when she caught the ball, but she seamlessly spun and put up a nifty fadeaway jumper that tickled the twine. The game was tied at two.

After a Hopkins three-pointer, another Wildcats turnover resulted in two easy points for the Royals. The Cats trailed 7–2.

The game was barely a minute old, but it already appeared the Royals were going to roll over the Wildcats. After Hopkins's press harassed Waconia into another turnover, the ball belonged to the Royals on the sideline, directly in front of Coach Neibauer. Neibs hollered out a reminder to his team about the play Hopkins preferred to employ when passing in from that position. Salsa took heed. Bueckers ran low along the baseline then cut up to the opposite wing to receive the ball. Salsa anticipated the pass and jumped in front of it for a clean steal. As she accelerated to the other end for what she thought would be a wide-open layup, a Hopkins defender came flying in from behind and blocked Salsa's shot, sending it into the Royals' student section. The block created such a roar from the home crowd that none of the fans noticed a foul had been called. Salsa was awarded two free throws. The junior guard made both and the score was 7–4 in favor of the home team.

Only two minutes of time had come off the clock when the first subs entered the game for Waconia. Ozzie, Raptor, and Mel replaced Snake, Bird, and Rookie. Neibs was looking to get a group on the floor that could better handle Hopkins's press. After a strong defensive possession resulted in a Hopkins turnover, Salsa brought the ball up the floor with the savvy and skill of a point guard. Bueckers shadowed her. In a move that Hopkins fans had seen Bueckers execute countless times, Salsa drove just inside the top of the key, and as additional Royals swarmed to stop her, she managed to maneuver the ball through the approaching onslaught of defenders to find a cutting Raptor at the rim for an easy layup. The pretty pass got a loud reaction from both teams' fans and it made the score 7–6 in favor of the Royals.

After a perfectly executed pick-and-roll put Hopkins up three, the Royals resumed their full-court pressure. The lineup Neibs inserted to counter the press did precisely what he had hoped. The ball was passed to Sauce. She promptly passed to Ozzie, who was cutting into the middle of the court. Then Ozzie stepped on the accelerator in a way she had not since her ACL injury. The backup point guard was a blur as she brought the ball down the floor. Bueckers was retreating and doing all she could to impede Ozzie's progress. The Wildcats were in a two-on-one fast break. All that stood between Ozzie and the basket was the best high school player in the country.

In a two-on-one, when the defender commits to the ball, the player with the ball is supposed to pass to her teammate. Ozzie had no plan to pass. The 5'6" Ozzie intended to take the ball right at the six-foot-tall UConn recruit. Ozzie never slowed down on her way to the hoop. She elevated the ball just beyond Bueckers's outstretched arm, bouncing it perfectly off the backboard to make the layup. Again the Waconia faithful cheered, and the Cats cut the lead to one.

Hopkins attempted a three on their next trip, but it missed the mark. Still intoxicated with adrenaline after scoring over the Royals' star player, Ozzie soared to secure the rebound. The backup point guard pushed the ball up the floor at a furious pace. When reaching the right wing, she was cut off by a Hopkins defender. As she was coached to do, Ozzie quickly passed the ball to the opposite side of the floor. Raptor caught it and rifled a pass to Salsa along the left baseline. Salsa dribbled the ball perilously close to the end line as she attempted to advance her way to the hoop. She had snuck behind the backboard, and in that moment, the Hopkins defenders let down their guard. That's when Salsa took one more dribble, contorted her body in midair, and converted a layup as she was fouled. With four minutes gone, the Wildcats had taken a 10–9 lead. The Waconia fans were going wild. As Salsa stepped to the free-throw line, Sauce could hear Paige Bueckers yelling at her teammates, "We've got to quit fouling!" Sauce felt a degree of satisfaction knowing her Wildcats were making the top-ranked Royals nervous.

Salsa missed the free throw, and a moment later Hopkins took back the lead. After their made basket, the Royals' full-court press suddenly had an additional urgency to it. Less than a minute later Hopkins was ahead 17–10. With 12 minutes remaining in the first half, Bird cut down the lane on a baseline out-of-bounds play and scored a layup to make a small dent in the growing Hopkins margin. The Cats trailed 23–12. Three minutes later Hopkins was in the midst of a 29-to-4 run and they extended the lead to 38–14.

When the Wildcats walked into the locker room at halftime, they were on the wrong end of the 65–29 score. Oddly the team was not distraught. Neibs was a little annoyed that somewhere in the midst of the Hopkins blitz his players seemed to have transitioned from competing to being starstruck. Dusty was adamant that the Wildcats must continue to compete and play hard. He tried to put a positive spin on things by reminding them they were facing what "basically amounts to a D-I college team."

Coach Neibauer continued, "So every time you score in the second half, celebrate it. You are scoring against a D-I college team. Every time we stop them, celebrate it. You demonstrated the ability to defend a D-I college team."

When the horn sounded to signal the end of the game, Hopkins had prevailed 101–57. Waconia was certainly sore, but they had lifted the heaviest weight in the state and they knew they would be stronger for it.

Hopkins continued their undefeated streak for the rest of the season and went on to be named High School National Champions by ESPN. But for four fantastic minutes at the start of the game, the Waconia Wildcats were better than the best high school basketball team in America.

The Cats had a lot of fun on social media in the days immediately following the Hopkins game. An Instagram feed with more than three million followers (@Overtime) posted highlights. People from all over the country were watching Paige Bueckers make jaw-dropping behind-the-back passes and they were watching her do those things to the Wildcats. Some of the Waconia girls were getting roasted in the site's comments section. Though a national audience was having fun at their expense, the girls got a laugh out of it and took it in stride.

While two lopsided losses were not how they had hoped to start the season, the Wildcats were buoyed by the knowledge they would have a chance to win their next two games. Roseville and Lakeville South were good AAAA teams, but they weren't national champion material or even among the top 10 in their class. Dusty was desperate to win at least one of the next two games. If he didn't, he knew there was a real chance his team would head into the holiday break with only one win and six losses.

The games would be played on a Friday and Saturday as part of an annual post-Thanksgiving invitational at historic Hamline University in St. Paul. Hamline proudly proclaims itself the "birthplace of college basketball." The story goes that four years after James Naismith invented the game, one of Naismith's original teammates arrived at Hamline and started a team. The first official game between two college basketball teams took place in 1895. Hamline handled the University of Minnesota Agricultural School by a score of 9–3.

Fast-forward to the 1920s. Hamline had become a hotbed of basketball in the upper Midwest. To accommodate their growing fan base, the university built an arena in 1937. The facility was ahead of its time. It featured long wooden bleachers on either side of the main court with room to seat 2,000. A balcony level offered additional bleacher seating for another 1,000 fans. There was an indoor track that wrapped around the backside of the bleachers and beyond both ends of the basketball court. Legend has it there were even secret apartments above the balcony reserved for star players such as future Minneapolis Laker and NBA Hall of Famer Vern Mikkelsen.

The arena was eventually named after one of the legendary coaches in Hamline history, Joe Hutton. The first game played in the new facility pitted the Pipers (yes, their mascot was a kilt-wearing Scotsman blowing bagpipes) against West Coast power Stanford University. To provide a bit more perspective, the first NIT tournament was played a year later, in 1938. The first NCAA tournament was held in 1939. Hutton Arena was filled with fans and played host to marquee games before those celebrated events even existed. Hamline was a place brimming with basketball history. Waconia had played there before, and the girls always appreciated the feeling of stepping back in time when they walked onto the court.

Neibs had a different feeling as his team trotted onto the floor for warm-ups: trepidation. During his preparation for first-round opponent Roseville, Neibs received a special warning from one coach. "They are a bunch of bruisers, but especially watch out for No. 41—she's crazy." The coach claimed that the Roseville forward had bitten one of his players in the teams' matchup the previous season. The fact that Roseville was famously such a physical squad made Neibs even more nervous. Teams that pushed and shoved tended to be tough for the Cats to overcome.

With the game about to begin, the crowd at Hutton Arena was sparse. Neibs looked at Sizzle, Cee Cee, and the rest of his reserves and said, "You guys are gonna have to give us energy today. We can't rely on the fans to get us going."

It was the Wildcats' third game of the season, and for the third consecutive game Waconia started slow. Roseville took advantage. The Raiders built a 13–4 lead in the opening minutes. Coach Neibauer's sense of urgency was becoming palpable and started to imbue his players. As their coach became increasingly animated and enthusiastic, the Cats clawed their way back to take a brief lead late in the first half, but the team trailed 27–26 at intermission.

The first half had been every bit as physical as advertised. The officials had elected to look the other way on most of the pushing and poking. Before leaving the locker room for the second half, Neibs reminded the team they needed to adjust to the officiating. If the refs were going to let a lot of stuff go, the girls needed to get more physical.

Snake took Coach Neibauer's comments to heart. On the Wildcats' first possession of the second half, Rookie launched a long three-point attempt. Snake crashed into the paint preparing for a rebound. When Snake arrived at her destination, a Roseville player had beaten her to the spot, so Snake put both of her hands on the defender's back and shoved the girl to the ground. The rebound came off the rim right to Snake, who promptly put it back up for an easy two points. Waconia was back in the lead, 28–27.

As the Raiders returned to offense, they missed an easy layup opportunity. Bird grabbed the rebound and dribbled up the floor. When she crossed halfcourt, Bird noticed Rookie ready and waiting at the top of the key. The stripe to mark the college men's three-point line was noticeably farther back than the high school three-point line. Rookie was a full step behind the college men's line when she caught the pass. A true shooter, the blonde bomber didn't hesitate. She drained the long-distance shot to extend her team's lead to four.

Seconds later Snake used her fast hands to knock the dribble away from the Roseville point guard. As Snake galloped in for a layup, Roseville got their revenge. As Snake elevated for the shot, a blatant retaliatory shove in the back sent her crashing to the floor. Again the officials swallowed their whistles. The game had officially eroded into a street fight.

For the next several minutes, bodies from both teams were banging against the floor. Only in the most egregious of circumstances was anyone whistled for a foul. Historically this kind of contest had ended in a Wildcats defeat. Instead, in this game that would have passed for pro wrestling had there been turnbuckles on the corners of the court, Waconia was actually extending its lead. With a little more than five minutes remaining, the Cats were up 53–41. The lead was still a comfortable nine points with fewer than two minutes left. But Roseville was not the type of team to go down without a fight.

The Raiders made a three with 1:50 remaining to trim the Waconia lead to six. After Bird missed a runner in the lane, Roseville was fouled as they grabbed the rebound. In the "bonus," they would be able to walk to the other end to shoot free throws. Converting one of two, the Waconia lead was reduced to five at 58–53. It was the Wildcats' ball with 1:35 left.

Minnesota does not have a shot clock for high school basketball; however, that was another unique thing about the Hamline

Invitational: all games were played with the 35-second college shot clock. If the game had been played under normal circumstances, the Wildcats would have held the ball and forced Roseville to foul them. Instead the shot clock was mandating that Waconia put up a shot or automatically forfeit possession.

With the shot clock nearly exhausted, Snake caught the ball in the corner, directly in front of the Wildcats bench. When she released the shot, a Roseville player came crashing in from the side, attempting to block the shot. Snake was knocked to the ground in the process. Despite a demonstrative plea for a foul by Coach Neibauer, the officials looked the other way once again. Roseville grabbed the rebound and went on the attack. After a long pass up the floor, one of the Raiders was making a beeline for the basket. Raptor had hustled to beat the Roseville player to the block. The Raiders guard showed some stellar footwork, walking right past Raptor for a layup to whittle the Wildcats' lead to three.

Roseville attempted to launch into a full-court defense. The Wildcats passed the ball in so quickly the Raiders' press was never able to materialize. Salsa brought the ball down the middle of the floor and found Snake wide-open at the right block. The senior captain banked the ball off the glass and Waconia was back in front by five with 52 seconds left. Roseville called timeout.

Neibs was closing in on his first win as varsity coach…kind of. Before stepping into the role full-time, Dusty had three previous opportunities to call the shots as "acting head coach." In his first year as JV coach, the varsity coach's wife went into labor on the last day of the regular season. With the head coach gone at the hospital, Neibs guided the team that night. The Cats lost a close contest. A few years later, the head coach got ejected arguing a call in the final minute of a very intense game. Minnesota State High School League rules stipulate that if a player or coach is ejected from a game, he or she must sit out the next game. As a result, Neibs took the reins as the team won in a blowout against a conference opponent. While that may have unofficially been his first win as a head coach, Neibs knew how important it would be to hang on to this lead and get a *W* given the brutally tough schedule that made up the first month of the season.

During the timeout, Neibs's demeanor and tone were tense. After reminding the team of the shot-clock situation, the coach explained that if there were fewer than 35 seconds and the Cats were still in the lead, they did not have to shoot. The team broke the huddle in the same way they had for years. Neibs yelled out, "Team on one!" Then a captain would call out "One!" and the rest of the players would instantly respond with "Team!"

Over the next 20 seconds of action, a sequence of free throws by the Wildcats and three-point baskets by Roseville whittled the Waconia lead down to a single point. With 22 ticks left on the clock, the Cats had the ball under their opponent's basket. Sweat was visibly gathering on Coach Neibauer's forehead. He used his sleeve to wipe the perspiration away.

Unable to pass the ball in against Roseville's full-court pressure and in danger of a five-second violation, Neibs screamed for a timeout just before the whistle would have awarded the ball to the Raiders. The coach sent Mel to the scorer's table to sub in for post defensive specialist Dozer. Dusty made the move due to Mel's superior ball-handling and free throw–shooting skills. Then, with the players leaning in to listen, Neibs explained that whoever caught the inbounds pass did not need to dribble. Roseville would be forced to foul them. "Just hold on to the ball and protect it" were his final words as the team broke the huddle.

Salsa was assigned to pass the ball in. Roseville took full advantage of the permissive officiating, holding and grabbing at the other four Wildcats as they attempted to get open. The Raiders were making it almost impossible for Salsa to find a passing lane. Finally Salsa managed to get the ball to Mel. The junior guard was promptly fouled. Mel, the girl who had been stuck on the JV team the season before, the player who was not sure she wanted to continue her basketball career, was now being counted on to make clutch free throws with 15 seconds left in a one-point game. Neibs held his breath as his former JV star stepped to the line. Mel's first free throw kissed the left side of the rim before rolling around and falling in. Dusty exhaled an audible sigh of relief. The lead was two, but a two-point advantage was not enough to bring Coach Neibauer's blood pressure back down to a healthy level. The coach was acutely aware of the numerous ways his team could still lose the game. Only a three-point lead would eliminate the threat of a last-second loss.

On the second free-throw attempt, the iron was not as kind. Mel's shot missed, and in the battle for the rebound, Raptor was knocked to the ground as Roseville grabbed the ball. With Raptor dazed and disoriented after being dropped to the hardwood, the

Raiders were able to attack in a five-on-four fast break, trailing by two with time running out. Neibs's nightmare scenario was now in play. A three-point shot at the buzzer could cost the Cats a game they desperately needed to win.

After advancing the ball up the floor, the Roseville point guard slowed down for a moment, attempting to alter her path by dribbling to the other side of the floor. Alone on the other end of the court, Raptor had risen up and was racing to get back on defense. The Raiders point guard had her back turned and was oblivious to the fifth Waconia defender who was rapidly approaching from behind. The savvy sophomore Raptor took advantage by poking the unsuspecting point guard's dribble away. With only eight seconds left, the loose ball came to rest in Snake's hands. Had the senior captain simply held on to the ball as her coach had instructed, it would have essentially ended the game. Instead Snake instinctively started to dribble. This allowed the Raiders one last opportunity.

On Snake's second dribble, a Roseville player darted up and stole the ball back. The Raiders thief drove down the lane for what would be the game-tying score. In an attempt to atone for her turnover, Snake sprinted into the paint, forcing the Raider to halt her assault. Prevented from a clear path to shoot, the ball handler spotted a teammate standing alone in the narrow area between the arc of the three-point line and the Roseville team bench.

The Raider zipped a pass to her open teammate, who launched the potential game-winning shot one second before the buzzer sounded. While the ball arced toward the hoop, Neibs and the Wildcats were frozen. After 35 minutes and 59 seconds of intense action, they were now helpless to affect the outcome of the game while they watched the ball continue on its journey. It was only the third game of the year, but in that moment, it felt like the season hung in the balance as they waited for the ball to begin its downward descent. An 0–3 start, especially after blowing what had been a nine-point lead with fewer than two minutes left, could send the Cats into a negative spiral from which they may never recover. All of that was racing through their minds in the seeming eternity it took for the ball to finally reveal their fate. Mercifully it bounced off the back of the rim just after the buzzer sounded. The Wildcats had escaped with their first victory of the season.

Scrunchie and Snake led the scoring with 12 points apiece. Raptor collected her first career double-double, netting 11 points to go with 10 rebounds. And Neibs got his second career win as a varsity coach, though it felt like his first.

After the game, the verdict was unanimous: it had been the most violent, physical game any of the girls had ever participated in. Ozzie may not have led the team in scoring, but a quick look at the backup point guard's arms and legs suggested she likely led the team in bruises. The Wildcats had no time to lick their wounds. There was another Class AAAA foe looming in fewer than 24 hours.

When the team gathered at Waconia High School to walk through Lakeville South's offense and to discuss their players' tendencies, everyone was well aware that Snake was only six points shy of 1,000 for her career. There was a sense of anticipation that history would happen that day. In the forty-five year "modern era" of the girls basketball program, only six players had made it to the milestone. Neibs was aware that Snake was closing in, but for the moment, his focus was on Lakeville South.

"They keep their shooters in the corners and they want to drive and kick out to them," Neibs advised. "No. 11 stays planted in the high post and she sets a lot of screens for their guards. Sauce, Scrunchie, and Dozer are going to have to hedge hard or their guards will be able to waltz into the lane for a layup."

Most of Neibs's instructions had evaporated from Snake's mind by the time the team boarded the bus. Even though she had scored more than six points in nearly every game of her varsity career, there was something about history and the way it hovered over her that made this game feel different from all the rest.

When the Wildcats came out for warm-ups, there was a bigger crowd at Hutton Arena than there had been the day before. Maybe it was because people were now two days removed from Thanksgiving. Families said their traditional long Minnesota goodbyes on Friday, so Saturday was open for an excursion to the cities. Or perhaps the additional audience was there because the word had circulated around Waconia that Snake was only six points away from history. Whatever the reason, the stands were noticeably more full than they had been on Friday.

As the game tipped off, an unsettling trend became evident. The Wildcats were off to a slow start for a fourth consecutive game. Lakeville South owned the opening minutes and built a 15–7 advantage. However, Waconia controlled the rest of the half. The Cats outscored the Cougars 27–9 over the final 14 minutes and carried a comfortable 34–24 lead into the locker room at halftime. Forced to the bench for a long stretch due to foul trouble, Snake had only managed to net two points in the first half. Her teammates were still certain she would reach the monumental mark that day. With every second that melted off the clock, Snake was feeling more anxious that she would fall short.

There are so many people here, she thought to herself as she emerged from the halftime huddle. *My friends drove here and made signs.*

It is often said the only pressure that really exists is that which we apply to ourselves. With thoughts of disappointing her fans and friends consuming her, the usually subdued, unflappable Snake was doing a better job of playing defense on herself than the Cougars were.

Waconia continued to control the game well into the second half, but fouls were becoming a factor. The Cats lead was seven with eight minutes to play when Neibs was forced to sit several starters in an effort to make sure they would be available at the end of the game. Sauce and Salsa were all who remained of the first five. Like any good predators, the Cougars recognized weakness and pounced. Fewer than two minutes after the Wildcats starters sat down, Lakeville South made a layup to knot the score at 49. The cheers of the Cougars fans filled historic Hutton Arena. The momentum was clearly with Lakeville South. Then something odd happened.

When the Cougars' game-tying shot went through, it did so with such velocity that the net snapped upward and part of the nylon got caught by a hook on the rim. The officials had to stop the game to extricate the net from its temporary cage. One of the referees began throwing the ball up at the net in an attempt to free it from the hook. During his multiple attempts, the Lakeville South crowd, so raucous and rowdy only seconds earlier, became quiet. All the fans were transfixed as the ref continued to toss the ball up toward the net. Finally, on his sixth try, the net was knocked free. Fortunately for Waconia, the Cougars' momentum had also escaped. With six minutes to go and the score tied, it was anybody's game.

When play resumed, the ball belonged to Waconia. After a few seconds of passing around the perimeter, Sauce conjured up some "midrange magic," making a jump shot at the junction of the free-throw line and the lane to propel the Cats back into the lead.

Moments later Salsa stole the ball and passed it across the floor to Ozzie. The dynamic junior point guard sped up the left side of the floor and found Dozer alone at the right block. Ozzie delivered a perfect pass and Dozer banked it off the board to extend the lead to four.

Saddled with four fouls, Snake was cheering loudly from the bench. She had made a free throw early in the second half, but Snake was still three points shy of 1,000. With three and a half minutes left and the lead still at four, Neibs sent his foul-plagued starters to the scorer's table to check in.

After empty possessions for both teams, Bird had the ball on the right wing. She passed to Snake at the top of the key. Immediately Snake attacked the lane with her left hand. She tossed up a floater with her right hand and was hit by a Cougars defender at the height of her jump. The basket was good! Snake would also be awarded a free throw, and with it, the chance to become part of a club only six other players in program history had membership in. Lakeville South would force Snake to ponder her place in history for a bit longer. They asked for a timeout.

As Snake sat down for the 60-second break, her teammates couldn't contain their excitement. Neibs also acknowledged what was waiting when they emerged from the huddle.

"First of all, Snake…no pressure," Neibs said as he flashed a big grin. "If you make this and reach a thousand points, that will be really awesome." Then Neibs turned his attention to the team and continued, "Whether she makes this or misses it, it doesn't change the fact that we need to get back on defense and get a stop. We are at a crucial point in this game." Neibs then reminded the team about the way their opponent had rallied in the closing seconds the day before. He announced there would be "time to celebrate Snake's accomplishment after the game, but right now we need to stay focused."

Snake didn't appreciate Neibs's playful reminder of what her pending free throw represented. She was already almost over-whelmed by the pressure. The logical part of Snake's brain was trying to remind her that there were plenty of games left. She would certainly make it to the mark. However, as Snake stepped to the line, her logic was being drowned out by the roar of the Waconia fans. She somehow managed to put all of the superflu-ous thoughts aside and focus only on the rim. It was one of the things that made Snake such a clutch performer throughout her career. She always had an ability to silence her mind when everything around her was chaotic. Snake took two dribbles and a deep breath, then let go of the shot. It went through the center of the cylinder, hitting nothing but net.

The Waconia fans exploded. Despite Dusty's insistence that there would be time to celebrate after the game, the players on the bench could not contain their jubilance. Snake's 1,000th point had extended the lead to 56–49, but more than two minutes were left on the clock and the game was far from over.

With the milestone secured and any anxiety now absent, Snake returned to form and took over. The next trip down the floor, she again drove the lane and scored a twisting layup to extend the lead to eight. After South missed their next shot attempt, Salsa gathered the rebound and drove the ball up the court. She saw Snake sprinting down the side of the floor and fired a perfect pass. Snake caught the ball in stride and scored another layup to put the game out of reach.

After being stuck at three points for what felt like forever, Snake scored seven of the Wildcats' last nine points to propel her team to another important win and to secure her place in the Waconia record book.

It was an exuberant postgame locker room with much to celebrate. The players were proud they had posted wins against good AAAA opponents and excited to see Snake make history. Most notably for Neibs, the team had evened its record to 2–2, the absolute best he could have hoped for as they reached the halfway point in their running of the gauntlet.

In the midst of all the celebratory smiles and laughter, there was one Wildcat withholding her true feelings. Sauce was sincerely happy for her teammates' big moment and glad that her team had won. As a captain, she knew the team's success had to be her primary focus. Even with that understanding, Sauce couldn't help feeling confused and frustrated. The three-year starter and senior captain had not been on the floor for the final minutes of the win over Roseville. Now, in the victory over Lakeville South, when Snake and the other starters returned to the court with three minutes remaining, Sauce had been subbed out and resigned to the role of spectator.

A long-established varsity regular, Sauce was left to wonder if she was doing something wrong. What had led her coach to lose confidence in her? Sauce recognized that as a team captain, she couldn't demonstrate any disappointment after her team's big win, so she suppressed her pain and continued to wear a smile.

After the team bus got back to Waconia, Sauce drove home and opened up to her parents about the way being banished to the bench made her feel. "Am I doing something wrong?" she asked out loud. With two parents who had competed collegiately, Sauce didn't find the level of sympathy she was seeking.

"You obviously need to practice harder," her dad advised.

"Scrunchie and Raptor are better than you," her mom added.

Sauce knew her mom was right. She knew the two talented sophomores were better. It was just hard for her to accept.

Her dad's suggestion that she needed to practice harder was what hurt the most. Sauce reflected on all the time the two of them had spent in the gym at St. Joe's. She knew the only player on the team who devoted more time to improving was Salsa. Sauce stewed thinking about how she found time to shoot five days a week all throughout the off-season, how she was the person who set up all of the team's open gyms. Sauce knew that if it weren't for her, at least half of her teammates would have been sitting on a couch instead of sharpening their skills for a state tournament run. That is why even though she acknowledged the sophomores were better, it was going to be hard for her to accept a reduced role.

Plus, even if Scrunchie and Raptor were better, that didn't explain the end of the Roseville game. When Scrunchie fouled out with a few minutes to go, Neibs didn't turn to his starter and senior captain. He subbed in Dozer for the stretch run. Though Sauce continued to be upset and confused, she decided she would have to keep those feelings to herself. Her team had won two in a row. As a captain, she had to keep her focus on the team.

Having played four games in the season's first seven days, the Cats finally had a chance to catch their breath. There were only three games on the schedule over the course of the next 20 days. In Coach Neibauer's view, the first four opponents had called attention to some of the team's weaknesses. The coach considered the next three weeks a great opportunity to focus on improving in a few specific areas. The players were not nearly as enthused about the prospect of 12 practices and only 3 games during the three-week window.

Their aversion to practice stemmed from a feeling that Neibs talked too much. The players felt like they spent more time standing around rather than doing drills or scrimmaging. For a new coach trying to implement novel concepts, it can take longer to explain how things are supposed to function. It turns out the team wasn't terribly interested in learning new things. They were a veteran group who had experienced success. While the players were becoming increasingly frustrated with what they considered stagnant practices, Dusty's own frustrations with practice were starting to fester. He felt like the players weren't "buying in" to the way he wanted to do things. Neibs thought the girls were giving a half-hearted effort in practice. He worried that lack of effort would eventually cost them a game. Then along came the Jefferson High School Jaguars from Bloomington, Minnesota.

Once a proud program, the Class AAAA Jaguars had fallen on hard times. They lacked consistency in their coaching staff and the number of girls coming out for the team had been in steady decline. Waconia had handled them easily the season before. Dusty and the team had every expectation they would win this matchup as well. When the Wildcats arrived at Jefferson's gym and learned the Jaguars' roster was so thin they would have several of their JV players getting major minutes in the varsity game, the outcome seemed a foregone conclusion. The Cats coasted to a 58–25 halftime lead. The lead remained so large, the JV team got major minutes during the second half. That meant forgotten senior Will would get a chance to shine in a varsity game. Her teammates cheered when Will sank a three-pointer to get the Wildcats' point total to the century mark. Mercifully the game ended moments later and Waconia walked off with a lopsided 103–45 win.

Continuing a tradition that had started the season before, after every game, no matter the outcome, Neibs would award one player with a rock. He had painted thirty-two rocks in the team colors of purple, white, and gold and placed them in a large glass jar. Thirty-two because that was the number of games the Cats would play if they made it all the way to the state championship. There were two main motivations for the jar of rocks. The overall impetus was to provide players with a clear visual of how much time was left in their season. By February the team would inevitably notice the once-full jar was now nearly devoid of rocks. Players would reach the realization that time was running out that they needed to get geared up to finish the season strong.

The rocks also offered a chance to recognize a player who had demonstrated remarkable effort to help the team in a particular game. Sometimes the rock went to the leading scorer. Sometimes it was awarded to a JV player who had done an excellent job of preparing the varsity to defend an opponent. No matter who it went to, receiving the rock was always considered an honor.

After addressing the team about the game, Neibs's final act was always the announcement of the rock. He would call out the player's name and then proclaim, "You rock!" as he handed the athlete the symbolic trophy. It meant a lot to Will when she was presented with the rock after the Jefferson game. The forgotten fourth senior had taken advantage of her opportunity to shine. In that moment, with her teammates cheering her on, Will felt recognized and appreciated for her efforts. She felt important to the team. It was a happy bus ride home.

Coach Neibauer was not able to enjoy the win for long. He understood that such a convincing victory would only exacerbate the lack of intensity already pervasive at practice. The frustration he had been suppressing over what he perceived as a lack of urgency from his players was about to boil over.

When Waconia looked at their next opponent, St. Michael–Albertville High School, it was as though they were looking 10 years into the future. STMA, as they were more commonly and succinctly known, had followed the same arc as Waconia. Years before, St. Michael and Albertville were two towns so small that they had consolidated into a single school district. Located 35 miles northwest of the Twin Cities and directly on the path of Interstate 94, St. Michael and Albertville didn't stay little for long. The towns and their schools had seen such explosive growth that the new high school they had opened in 1992 was obsolete just 16 years later. Another new, even larger high school had to be built in 2008. STMA had climbed the ladder from Class AA to Class AAA, and now they had spent the past decade rising up the ranks in the state's largest class, AAAA. When the STMA Knights walked into Waconia High School they carried the No. 6 ranking in Class AAAA with them.

After five road games to begin the schedule, it was the Wildcats' first home game of the season. A nice crowd had come to get their first glimpse of their highly touted hometown team. The Wildcats were aware that STMA was a good team, but after watching video, they also believed the Knights could be beaten. That belief was rapidly challenged in the game's opening minutes.

It felt like Waconia was reliving the season opener against Rosemount. STMA sprinted to a 12–0 lead and never looked back. By the time the score was 21–3, the Waconia players were feeling a degree of embarrassment both on the court and on the bench. The home crowd had come expecting to see one of the best teams in Class AAA. The talk around town was that *this* Wildcats team would be the one to reverse the curse and finally get to state. Waconia fans had to wonder if they had been misled as they sat in awkward silence, watching their Wildcats be slayed by the Knights. The players fretted that their fans would lose faith.

The visitors were up 49–20 at intermission. Several of the disappointed spectators took the 10-minute interlude as an opportunity to get a head start on their drive home. When the Wildcats returned to the floor to start the second half, they couldn't help but feel hurt to find the bleachers mostly barren, as more than half of their fans had given up on the game.

The STMA lead swelled to 40 early in the second half. Minnesota may not have a shot clock, but it does have a mercy rule. When a team leads by 35 or more with nine minutes or fewer left in the game, the clock goes to running time. A few days earlier, the Cats had been on the right side of a running-time game. This night, in their long-awaited and much-anticipated home opener, they were decidedly on the wrong end. The final score was 84–45.

After the game Neibs entered the somber locker room and unloaded. The frustration he had been bottling up about his team's lack of enthusiasm and energy at practice had reached a boiling point. The girls had never seen him like this. His face was flushed red. His eyes were squinted in an aggressive glare. As loud as it was, the coach's yelling was still not overwhelming enough to disguise his obvious angst.

As the JV coach, Neibs was almost always jovial. He was fun and a lot more laid-back. Things have a tendency to change when you are the one being held accountable for the performance of a team that entered the season with lofty expectations. Perhaps the large home crowd and the lackluster performance by his team had embarrassed Dusty to a degree as well. What was not in doubt was that the coach was not content with the way his team had competed that night, nor did he find their effort in practice to be acceptable. After a few minutes of unburdening himself, Neibs and the coaching staff left. The players had been scolded. The locker room was uncharacteristically quiet as the team changed out of their uniforms and got ready to head home.

There were six consecutive practices before the final game of the gauntlet. That meant there were six chances to demonstrate the focus and intensity their coach had demanded with such emotion after the disappointing home debut.

Dusty's postgame diatribe may have improved the players' focus at practice for a day or two, but after that, he noticed no discernible difference. The coach was concerned his team would take another beating at the hands of Chaska, the No. 9–ranked team in AAAA. Chaska was one of the closest towns to Waconia. Like Victoria and Chanhassen, it was little more than 10 miles away, marking the outer edge of the Twin Cities suburbs. Proximity meant the teams played almost every season. In what had been a consistently competitive series, the home team had won the last four meetings. This year it was the Wildcats' turn to host in what would be the final game for both teams before their schools went on winter break. Dusty was hopeful that if his team wasn't able to pull off the upset, then at a minimum they would put up a fierce fight and be able to head out for the holidays on a positive note.

While the Cats once again trailed from the opening tip, they did not dig themselves a double-digit hole like they had done against the other AAAA foes. Through the first 18 minutes of action, the team never trailed by more than five. At halftime Chaska nursed a narrow 33–32 lead.

Dusty and the players were very positive at halftime, pleased with their effort and execution in the initial 18 minutes. The second half unfolded very differently. The Hawks outscored the Wildcats 33–11 in the first 10 minutes and the Chaska lead ballooned to 23. Waconia rallied a bit at the end to make the final score look more respectable, but when the team walked into the locker room after the game, their attitudes were decidedly different. They were downtrodden. Dusty was as disappointed as the players, but he knew he couldn't chew them out again. Everyone would be going their separate ways for a full week after his postgame comments. Neibs had to find a way to send them out on a positive note.

"We competed with one of the best teams in AAAA for a full half. That's progress," Dusty said. "And we missed about a dozen close shots. Finish around the rim and we could have been up at halftime by 10 or 12!"

He continued, "It seemed like we came out for the second half satisfied that we were in the game instead of hungry to win it. We competed for a long period of time against a good team. Tonight was part of learning to compete. The season is a long journey. I don't expect that any of us likes the outcome, but we took a step in the right direction tonight."

Dusty did his best to send his team into the holidays on a high note.

The girls were left unconvinced.

This time when the coaches walked out of the locker room, the players were far from silent. Trouble was brewing.

CHAPTER 7

A Dark December

In the most literal sense, December's days are the darkest of any basketball season. The month's shorter days and longer nights are an inescapable truth of winter. Minnesota is by no means Alaska, where in some of the cities furthest north, the sun literally disappears for several weeks. However, Minnesota may as well be Alaska for basketball players and coaches, because when they arrive at school in the morning, the sun has yet to send even a hint of its comforting crimson colors over the horizon. By the time the teams climb back into their cold cars after practice, the sun has long since retreated and the only light the players and coaches will see is the dull yellow glow of the streetlamps lining the road or the occasional twinkle of a home adorned with Christmas lights.

The houses covered in blinking bulbs of white, red, and green act as a reminder of one of the other big challenges brought about by the basketball season: the tremendous toll it takes on time spent with family. Never is that more noticeable than around the holidays. There is little opportunity to linger at Grandma and

Grandpa's house for an extra day because another game or tournament is always in the offing. Such was the case for the Wildcats this season. With barely a chance to digest their Christmas dinner, the team was back in the gym early on the morning of December 26 preparing for a game that afternoon.

Hill-Murray, a private high school just outside of St. Paul, had hosted a high-profile eight-team holiday tournament for years. This was the first time the Wildcats had competed in the event. Their first-round matchup was against another school from the suburbs of St. Paul, Henry Sibley High School. Named after the first governor of Minnesota, Henry Sibley was a school like Waconia, on the bubble between being the smallest school in AAAA but still among the biggest in AAA.

The varsity game was scheduled for 3:00 PM, but the bus would depart from Waconia High School at 8:00 in the morning because the JV team was scheduled to play in an auxiliary gym at 9:00 AM. The varsity players had to report to the gym at 7:00 AM to complete their walk-through of Henry Sibley's offense. Then they grudgingly boarded the bus five hours earlier than they would have liked. When the JV game was over, there were at least four hours before the varsity needed to be in the locker room getting ready for their game. Anticipating the extended downtime between games, Neibs had hatched a plan to keep the team busy and hopefully do a little team-building too.

The girls ate an early lunch, then the bus took the team to a bowling alley. It was a desolate place the day after Christmas; it was almost as if it were reserved for their private party. As the players grabbed their shoes and got ready to bowl, something caught Neibs's attention: All four seniors sat together at a lane. The five juniors joined up at another. The two sophomores, Scrunchie and Raptor, combined with some of the JV players into other lanes. The segregation by grade level caught his eye, but it was the absolute lack of interaction between each of the groups that the coach considered cause for concern.

There were a few laughs when someone threw a gutter ball and the obligatory cheers when a teammate rolled a strike, but Neibs had been around athletics long enough to know when a team genuinely enjoyed each other's company and when their interactions felt forced. The coach was getting a strong sense that his team was merely going through the motions.

When the first game concluded, Neibs announced the team had time to bowl another. The five juniors approached the coach and indicated they had had their fill. Then they asked if they could go out to the bus to sleep. Dusty didn't like the idea of the juniors separating themselves from the rest of the team. He was even more convinced that there was something bubbling below the surface. Despite his misgivings, Dusty decided to give the juniors the benefit of the doubt and he acquiesced. A possible problem was now on his radar, and the coach would keep a close eye on how the juniors responded to the rest of the team.

Even after an early morning and long day, the Wildcats made quick work of Henry Sibley, rolling to a 23-point triumph. The win advanced Waconia into the tournament semifinals against Mounds View High School. A mediocre AAAA school, the Mounds View

Mustangs were expected to provide minimal resistance and allow the Wildcats another win by a wide margin. Instead the Cats found themselves up only two at halftime. Waconia continued to sleepwalk through most of the second half. With a bit more than five minutes to go in the game, the Wildcats found themselves trailing the less-than-formidable Mustangs by five.

Considering the deficit and the disappearing time, the Cats hadn't yet arrived in Panic City, but they were close enough to see the city-limits sign. The ball belonged to Waconia, who was trailing 52–47. Scrunchie caught a pass on the perimeter and was fouled as she drove the lane. She made the second of her two free throws to trim the deficit to four. Dusty took a timeout. He decided to have his team do something they rarely did: apply full-court defensive pressure. It was a decision derived from a sense of desperation, as the Wildcats were running out of time. Neibs also hoped the press would provide his team, which had largely played lethargically to that point, some life or a sort of spark.

Dusty's defensive adjustment worked. Mounds View was immediately rattled by the full-court defense. The Mustangs proceeded to force up an ill-advised shot that bounced out of bounds. With the ball back and a recognition that they needed to maximize each possession the rest of the way, Neibs called a play for Rookie. The sharp shooter delivered a big three-point basket and cut Mounds View's margin to one. Seconds later, a steal by Raptor culminated in a fast-break layup by Ozzie, and the Cats had climbed back on top.

The lead was short-lived. Mounds View dodged disaster with practically every pass, but they somehow managed to navigate the

Wildcats' full-court pressure. The Mustangs got a shot in the lane and scored the go-ahead basket. For the next two minutes, both teams came up empty on offense.

The scoring drought ended when Salsa slashed into the lane and drew a foul with 2:44 on the clock. The Wildcats were down one. The junior calmly cashed in both free throws to put the Cats back in front. Dusty ordered his defense to withdraw the press and retreat to the other side of halfcourt. Minus the full-court pressure, Mounds View was able to maneuver the ball to their best player, a lofty 6'3" center. She promptly swished a shot in the paint to make the score 56–55 in favor of Mounds View.

After a dead ball allowed subs to enter the game, Mel again found herself on the floor at crunch time. She brought the ball across halfcourt and saw Raptor making a backdoor cut. Mel, standing 30 feet away, threw a laser-like pass into the lane, where Raptor converted the easy layup. Moments later the Mustangs went back to their big post and she scored over Scrunchie's outstretched arms. With fewer than 90 seconds left, Waconia was down one and on the cusp of what would be a catastrophic loss. To fall to such an inferior team would damage the Cats tremendously when the time came to seed the section playoffs. It would also add fertilizer to the seeds of doubt that were already sprouting among so many players on the team.

The Cats had the ball out of bounds, under their basket, with 1:12 to play. Ozzie was scanning the court for an open player to pass to but having no luck. As the official was about to chop his hand for the fifth and final time, which would signal a five-second violation, Ozzie lobbed a desperation pass over the defense toward the top of the key. Raptor used every bit of her athleticism to make an acrobatic catch over the defender. The sophomore then rifled a pass to the left wing. Salsa was there to secure the ball with an empty lane in front of her. Salsa's left-handed layup put the Cats up by one with just more than a minute remaining.

In retrospect, what happened next should have been predictable because Waconia fans had seen her do it so many times, yet somehow it was still a wonderful surprise. Just after Mounds View brought the ball across halfcourt looking to regain the lead, Snake plucked the ball from the Mustangs point guard and accelerated to the other end for an easy layup, extending Waconia's edge to 61–58. Snake's venom had killed the Mustangs' chances and Waconia escaped with a win.

There's an old saying in the sports world that "winning makes a wonderful deodorant." However, the win didn't disguise the scent of dysfunction for Dusty. As the rookie head coach headed to the locker room, something still stunk.

In his postgame address to the team, Neibs said all of the obligatory things, such as, "We won't be able to simply show up and beat teams" and, "You came through when you had to, though." Then Dusty exited the locker room and turned to his trusted assistant, Ashley Westphal.

Westphal had been a popular teacher at WHS for 10 years. She had served as the head girls swimming coach for four of those. Westphal was a reasonably recent addition to the basketball staff, taking over the freshman team only the season before. Dusty's first act as head coach was to promote Ashley to the JV job he had previously occupied. Now he needed to lean on his top assistant for some reconnaissance.

Dusty explained his suspicions. He felt like there were some hard feelings and that factions were forming within the team. Neibs asked Coach Westphal to engage in some "casual conversation" with a couple players to see if she could uncover why the team seemed so out of sync. He didn't choose Westphal at random. He knew the girls had a great relationship with her and they would be more likely to open up about any issues to her than to him. Ashley accepted the mission and immediately went to work.

As the team slowly trickled out of the locker room, Coach Westphal noticed Raptor and Scrunchie chatting in a corner. She approached the two sophomores and in a nonchalant manner asked, "What's going on?"

"Nothing. Just talking about the game," Raptor replied.

"No. What's going on?" Westphal delivered the question more definitively this time.

After a long pause, Raptor responded, "Well, we just wanna win games, but players are talking lots of stuff about each other."

Ashley visited with the girls for only a minute more. A head coach herself, she had heard enough to diagnose the problem. The only question left unresolved was if the coaching staff could find a cure.

In her brief conversation, Westphal discovered the juniors had been complaining about a lack of leadership from the seniors. Certain players were being accused of deliberately not passing the ball to other players. Some players were upset that their scoring averages had dropped from where they had been the season before. There was also jealousy about how many minutes some players were getting versus others. The juniors were suggesting the five of them be subbed in together. When it was time for them to rest, the three main seniors should have a shift with the two sophomores. They claimed the "chemistry" of those groups would be better. So Neibs had been right in one regard: There was indeed a problem. The part he was not prepared for was his team being consumed with *multiple* problems.

On the 40-minute bus ride back to Waconia, Neibs and Westphal deliberated about what, if anything, they could do to get the team back on track. They determined there were only two courses of action. First, they could divorce themselves from the drama, effectively ignoring it. The coaches knew the Wildcats' schedule was far more favorable in January. Perhaps a long winning streak would bring an end to the internal conflicts. The second and more complicated course of action would be to convene the players for what was sure to be a tense team meeting filled with strong emotions.

As the bus pulled into the high school parking lot, Neibs had nearly forgotten his team had advanced to the championship game of the Hill-Murray Holiday Tournament and they would square off with the No. 2–ranked team in Class AAAA the following day. He had become transfixed by something bigger than any single game. The coach was convinced his team would never make it to state if they were divided. Neibs knew what he had to do.

Before the players stepped off the bus, Dusty declared, "Our 11 varsity players need to meet in my classroom an hour before the bus leaves tomorrow. The bus leaves at 4:00 PM. Varsity, I'll see you at three."

"Common spaces" are what they call the areas in between class-rooms at Waconia High School. Described in a much less clinical way, the areas are more reminiscent of a comfortable coffeehouse, complete with padded chairs and couches with some high-top tables interspersed throughout. It was in that area, just outside of his classroom, where Dusty had the players gather. As he had directed, they were all there promptly at 3:00.

"We have a game tonight, but we are not going to make it where we need to be, we aren't going to make it to state, if we don't address some issues first. What we are dealing with is bigger than one game." That is how Dusty started the discussion. He then addressed the issues that had been causing tension on the team: the senior/junior divide, the perception that people weren't passing to certain players, the petty jealousies that had been percolating.

Dusty's delivery became more passionate with each passing sentence. "I've been asking you to fight and battle against all of these top-ranked teams, but what I didn't realize is that we have also been battling ourselves. We've got two sophomores who are doing their own thing. Juniors who are saying seniors aren't leading them in the way they want and seniors who have no idea juniors feel this way because you don't talk to them!"

He paused and continued, "You've been ripping on each other instead of talking about these problems *with* each other. How many of you communicated with your teammates on the bench last game about what the defense is doing?" None of the players raised their hand.

"These issues are what I want you to talk about, but these are just suggestions by me. Collectively, as a team, you have to figure this out right now. I'm gonna go into my classroom and close the door. You tell me when I should come out. I will wanna know what you've discussed with each other and what you're going to do moving forward." With that, Dusty left the team to deliberate.

A little more than half an hour had passed when the players signaled they were ready. Coach Neibauer asked them what they had talked about. The captains spoke up and shared that everyone on the team knew they needed to practice harder and be more focused before games.

"No! You have ignored the most important part!" Dusty declared. "You can't skip over all the interpersonal stuff and just say, 'We're gonna practice harder.' That's not how this works!"

Dusty returned to his classroom. There were only 25 minutes before the bus would be taking the team to play in the holiday tournament championship, which is not a lot of time to resolve seemingly deep-seated issues.

Reluctantly the team started to tackle the tough topics. The seniors insisted they would solicit input and ideas from the younger players. The juniors acknowledged they had formed their own clique and resolved to mingle more with their teammates. The two sophomores sat in silence, deferring to their elders.

Then the forgotten fourth senior, Will, cleared her throat to get the team's attention and said, "This is a start. But there are other things that have led to these feelings. Our body language toward each other has been bad." Her teammates were nodding their heads in agreement. Will continued, "We have been losing sight of the larger goal. We need to quit complaining about who is taking shots or how many they are taking. We need to stop counting how many minutes we are playing versus our teammates." There could not have been a better, more credible player to deliver this import-ant message than Will. Every player on the team respected the way Will worked in practice and the unselfish attitude she brought to the bench.

"We can't control who is subbed into the game. We can't control how many shots our teammates take. We *can* control our body lan-guage. We *can* control the way we treat and talk about each other. Let's do those things right," she concluded.

Then Sauce spoke up and said, "We need to trust each other and remember that we are teammates, but we are friends first."

Snake added that she was glad the captains were now aware of how people felt and that they would do a better job moving forward. Then Snake adjourned the meeting by saying, "Now we need to put the drama aside and just play basketball."

The Wildcats were facing the Wayzata Trojans, who were a tall order...literally. They had a forward (not a post) who stood 6'4" and was adept at shooting threes. Wayzata was widely recognized as the only team in the state that could topple nationally ranked

Hopkins. Wayzata would be tough to beat, but this new, unburdened, more connected group of Wildcats was about to try.

After more than a month of chronically slow starts, the Wildcats were finally executing crisply at the beginning of the game. Through the first eight minutes of action, it appeared fans were in for a fun championship matchup. The underdog Wildcats were clicking and had built a 13–8 advantage. A few minutes later Wayzata took their first lead, but it was still competitive at 17–15. Then the No. 2–ranked Trojans went on a 24–12 run over the final five minutes of the half and they led 41–27 at the break.

The game was not over at intermission, but the size and skill of Wayzata was starting to win out. The Cats climbed back into the game briefly at the start of the second half, trimming the Trojans' lead to single digits. Then Wayzata pulled away. The final score was 88–55, though from Coach Neibauer's point of view, when his players opened up to each other and confronted the issues that had been corroding team chemistry, they had already won the day.

The Wildcats had run the gauntlet and emerged on the other side with a respectable record of 5–5. Neibs knew the squad had a favorable schedule in January. The coach could barely wait to get home, rip December off his calendar, and start a winning streak.

CHAPTER 8

Streaking

January is typically the coldest month of a Minnesota winter. Residents can routinely count on a stretch of 7 to 10 days where the high temperature never sneaks above single digits. This winter featured the rare January absent an arctic blast. For only five days in the entire month did the daytime high temp dip below a balmy 20 degrees above zero. In a month when Minnesota students commonly had school canceled for a day or two due to dangerously cold temperatures, Waconia students were coming to school without coats. Some of the boys with outrageously high metabolisms even walked in wearing shorts.

The only thing warmer than the unseasonable weather was the Wildcats. They started the new year with a 69–47 blowout win against Buffalo, handled rival Holy Family 71–55 in the Wright County Conference opener, and overwhelmed Orono by 21 points. The team's record rapidly improved to 8–5.

There was a setback when the team's primary three-point threat, Rookie, was diagnosed with pneumonia in the middle of the month. Though she wanted to battle through it, her physician insisted that she sit out for seven days. That meant Rookie would be sidelined for two games. Neibs knew the team would miss her ability to draw defenders out to the perimeter, thereby opening up opportunities for points in the paint. The coach also knew he had two sophomores who had performed in such an impressive manner they both merited "starter" status. In fact, with the team at precisely the midway mark of the regular season, the two youngest players on the team were leading the squad in scoring. Separated by only a point, Scrunchie was the team's leading scorer with Raptor right behind her. A closer look at the statistics showed the "super sophs" were not only leading the team in scoring; the dynamic duo were also ranked No. 1 and No. 2 in rebounding, with Scrunchie leading the way in that category as well. Dusty's dilemma was not that he needed to fill a starting spot for a few games; it was that he had two players who were worthy and he could only choose one.

After considering different combinations and mapping out how substitution patterns would be affected, it was Scrunchie who got the nod. Raptor would continue to come off the bench and provide the Wildcats with a lift. If there were any concerns about how the lineup change might affect the chemistry on the court, those worries were put to rest after a 92–75 win over neighboring AAAA school Chanhassen. In her first start, Scrunchie had game highs in points (23) and rebounds (13). Rookie, dressed in street clothes, watched from the end of the bench as her spot in the starting lineup looked like it might be disappearing.

After defeating Chanhassen, the Cats were not scheduled to take the court again for more than a week. During that stretch, the unseasonably mild Minnesota winter briefly reverted to its old ways. There was a major snowstorm in the forecast for Friday. In an effort to be proactive, the girls basketball game was moved up a day and Waconia hosted the Tigers of Delano on Thursday. Though heavy precipitation was not forecasted to fall for a few more hours, it was raining threes in the gym that night. Salsa led the team, scoring 17 points in a 24-point pasting of yet another conference opponent. The Waconia winning streak was now at five.

A few days later, when the snowplows had cleared a path, the Wildcats made the one-hour drive southwest to New Ulm. The game had postseason seeding implications, as the Eagles competed in Waconia's section. Again Scrunchie set the pace, pouring in 21 points and grabbing eight rebounds. Salsa and Raptor scored 11 points apiece. Rookie also added 11 in her first game back from illness. It was Rookie's first game reprising her role from the season before, being brought in off the bench as "instant offense."

It wasn't easy for her, but the famously positive Rookie resolved never to let her teammates know how much it hurt her to lose her starting spot. The only people she expressed her disappointment to were her mom and dad. In the presence of her teammates, Rookie kept smiling, though it was more forced than it had been before.

Rookie's coach had been working hard to hide something from the team too. With the holidays in the rearview mirror and the calendar flipped to January, it seemed some of the players' parents had made "Share my disappointment with the coach" one of their New

Year's resolutions. Every new coach enjoys a "honeymoon peri-od"—a window of time when players, parents, and fans are utterly optimistic about what the team can become under new leadership. Neibs had made it nearly six weeks into the season before he got his first angry parent email.

That first parent complaint is something of a rite of passage for any new head coach. Neibs had gone through the "gauntlet" and come out of it with 5 wins in 10 tries, but he did not emerge unscathed. The arrival of the angry email was the first tangible evidence that Dusty's honeymoon had come to an abrupt end.

A critical email will usually wound a new head coach to a greater degree than it would a veteran. Inexperienced coaches are already inclined to second-guess themselves and their decisions. When someone even peripherally associated with the program offers harsh criticism, it can send a rookie coach into a spiral of self-doubt. Dusty didn't get entirely sucked into that spiral by the email assault, but it clearly affected him.

While he didn't have the capacity to completely ignore the criticism, Dusty drew some degree of comfort from the fact his team was in the midst of a winning streak, and it was a dominant streak at that. No opponent had come closer than 17 points, and the team's average margin of victory during the streak was 22. Neibs was certain the continued success would ultimately silence his critics. Of course he was wrong. New coaches can possess a level of naïveté rarely seen in the natural world.

Legendary basketball coach Don Meyer once said, "A parent would rather see their kid win all-conference than win the conference championship." It is that dynamic that will forever complicate the relationship between coaches and parents. While a parent's only responsibility is to look out for the best interest of his or her child, a coach doesn't have the luxury of looking out for only one kid. A coach must always prioritize what is best for the team first and for individual players second. Though good coaches will always endeavor to do what is best for an individual, in the moment when what is best for one player comes into conflict with what is best for the team, to invoke Don Meyer once more, "That decision was made a long time ago." The coach must always put the team first. A parent will always put his or her kid first. That is why it rarely matters what a team's record is. Coaches will always be subject to criticism.

Dusty was able to extinguish the animosity that had been smoldering among his players by hosting an intervention before the championship of the Hill-Murray holiday tournament. However, the growing disgust from team parents was proving more difficult to douse. Over the next several days, additional emails arrived with the cliché complaints about playing time, about the type of offense the team was running, about playing "favorites." Those common criticisms were not that difficult for Dusty to dismiss. There was one line, though, in an isolated email, that had wounded him much more than the rest. When a parent declared Dusty's version of the Wildcats the most underachieving team they had ever seen, it struck a nerve. Like any rookie coach, Dusty had a healthy dose of self-doubt. Any confidence the winning streak had cultivated in him was erased with that single, scathing line from an angry parent's email.

After reading them, Dusty had let the emails sit in his inbox as he wondered what his next move should be. Should he respond to each accusation? Should he ask his athletic director for advice? Eventually Dusty decided the best course of action was to do nothing at all. He did not respond to the emails. However, he did respond to the pressure. Neibs struggled to sleep. His accelerating anxiety kept him awake until 1:00 or 2:00 AM every night. It wasn't until those wee hours of the morning that Dusty's body was so utterly overwhelmed with fatigue it finally forced him to fall asleep. During the handful of hours between his exhausted collapse and the alarm ordering him awake, basketball haunted his dreams. The coach's subconscious would transport him back to a moment in a game when he made a decision he regretted and force him to relive it.

For the first time in his 15-year coaching career, Dusty no longer looked forward to going to practice. He worried that if he said or did something wrong, more harsh words would find their way to his inbox. Dusty was doing his best to do the right thing. He was expending all of his waning energy in a single-minded effort to get his team to its first-ever state tournament, but the coach felt like he was under attack. And he felt alone.

Half of Neibs's four-person coaching staff was new. The only coach he had worked with whom he felt he could confide in was Coach Westphal. But Dusty kept the complaints away from his colleagues. He decided the criticism was his cross to bear. Like Rookie and Sauce, Dusty did his best to disguise how much he was hurting. Neibs tried to keep his focus on what was in front of him. There was always another practice to prepare for or another scouting report to write. Dusty didn't need angry emails to remind him of what he had done wrong. He was already tormented by past mistakes each night during his dreams in the miniscule minutes he managed to sleep.

In an effort to build on the progress made at the December team meeting, the girls had committed to gathering once a week outside of practice for some "team time." After beating Buffalo, the team congregated at Raptor's house. They ate, laughed, and talked late into the night. A week later they all hung out at Will's house for more of the same. The conversations rarely centered around basketball and instead were dominated by school, silly posts on social media, and boys. The casual team get-togethers seemed to be having the desired effect. The players weren't just seeing each other as teammates. It felt like they were cementing their friendship.

Like most high schools in Minnesota, Waconia did not have school on Martin Luther King Day. The seniors seized on another opportunity for "team time" and asked everyone to meet that morning for breakfast. With limited options in Waconia equipped to accommodate such a large group, the girls piled into cars and made the 10-mile drive to Chaska and the nearest Perkins. Seated together at a long table, they talked about the challenging classes they were taking, which teachers were the best (and worst), and though it was still more than three months away, there was some preliminary talk about prom. Then Snake interrupted with an idea.

"We should get a team fish!" she proclaimed. Her teammates laughed. "No, I'm serious! We should get a pet fish. We can keep it in the coaches' office in the locker room. It will be our team mascot!" The pet store across the parking lot from Perkins had almost certainly served as Snake's inspiration.

When it became clear their captain was serious, the players started to embrace the idea. After finishing their food, the squad sauntered across the parking lot in search of the fish they would adopt. Snake insisted the fish would give them good luck for the rest of the season. Armed with an acute awareness that their fish would be alone for most of the day, the girls committed to getting the most resilient fish they could find. They settled on a beta fish. Bird announced she already had an empty fish tank at home, so she paid for the fish and the food, then the team climbed into their cars and drove back to Waconia for practice. They were excited to introduce Neibs to the newest member of their team.

Sounding like a parent, Neibs explained it would be the players' responsibility to feed the fish and to change its water. The captains told him they would take care of it. The fish found a home just inside the window of the coaches' office, where the girls could collectively keep an eye on it. When practice was over, the Wildcats proudly posted pictures on social media of their new "o-fish-al" mascot.

Coaches will tell you that every game is important. The truth is, some games are more important than others. The home game on the horizon against the Hutchinson Tigers would be one of the biggest games of the season. Both teams had 11 wins. Both teams were in the hunt for the Wright County Conference championship. Perhaps most crucial of all, both teams resided in section two. That meant the winner of the game would have an upper hand when it came to seeding for the postseason.

Though they had started the season as the strong favorites to reach the state tournament, Waconia was squarely in the middle of the pack in the section standings as January was coming to a close. Section two's defending champions, the Marshall Tigers, were 15–0. It could be said they were a bit of a paper tiger, though, as many of their opponents were smaller schools in southwest Minnesota that didn't put up much of a fight. Mankato West and St. Peter were also keeping pace in the section standings with 11 wins apiece. Put succinctly, with the losses the Cats had accumulated in the outrageously challenging opening month of the season, the team had no margin for error if they wanted to be among the top seeds in the section tournament come March.

Hutchinson was known for their relentless, gambling defense. Like Marshall, Hutchinson's mascot was also a Tiger. It was a mascot that fit their style of play perfectly. Hutchinson's defense was famous for pouncing on young, inexperienced opponents and for ripping the ball away from weak or feeble guards. When Snake, Sauce, Bird, and Will were freshmen, the Tigers had trounced them. Now battle-tested veterans, the Wildcats were no longer easy prey.

The Waconia High School gym features 22 rows of long purple bleachers that extend 100 feet along both sides of the basketball court. The bleachers behind the team benches are reserved for visiting fans. Hutchinson had about a hundred fans travel the 40 miles to support their team in the crucial contest. The bleachers across from the benches were about 70 percent full of home fans excited to cheer on their red-hot Wildcats. Van Halen's 1984 anthem "Jump" blared through the public address system as the starters took their place around the center circle. In this collision of cats, it was the Tigers who drew first blood.

Hutchinson jumped out to a 5–2 lead, but it didn't take long before Waconia would take control. Over the course of the next five minutes, the Wildcats went on an 18–0 run to build an impressive 20–5 advantage. The Tigers rallied and trimmed the lead to eight. The Wildcats responded and built the lead back to 15. When the teams walked into the locker room to regroup, Waconia's lead was 11.

The Wildcats locker room features the same color scheme as the gym. Light gray walls are obscured by rows of prominent purple lockers. The players always filed into the locker room first. They would bunch together on the bench farthest from the door, arranged in such a way that they could each see the dry-erase board where the coaching staff would draw up any adjustments. While the coaches conferred in the hallway, Snake attempted to keep her teammates pumped up and intense. "We gotta act like we are down 11, not up 11. We can't let up!"

When the coaches came in, Neibs commended the team for their defensive intensity and for playing unselfishly. He also offered some words of warning. "Hutch is going to make a run. They are a good team. They are gonna make a run in the second half. How we respond to their run will determine the outcome." Neibs was relying on his years of experience as an assistant. He had seen Hutch make leads vanish in short order with their full-court pressure. Neibs knew it was important for his players to be mentally ready if the Tigers mounted a comeback.

The first 12 minutes of the second half made the coach's admonition seem meaningless. The Cats maintained a double-digit lead throughout. Salsa hit a jump shot on the baseline from 10 feet out to make the lead 57–44 with exactly six minutes to play. Then all at once the Wildcats came apart. Neibs's halftime warning was about to prove prophetic.

Hutch's shooters got hot, and every time they scored, the Tigers would leap into a frantic full-court press. The Wildcats had handled the torrent of Tigers pressure to that point, then inexplicably all five players in purple and gold began to panic simultaneously. With 3:45 on the clock, Hutchinson hit a three to tie the game at 58. The visitors had closed a 13-point gap in just more than two minutes. The Hutchinson bench and their 100 fans were jumping up and down and pumping their fists with excitement at the sudden turn of events. The momentum was clearly on the Tigers' side.

With Hutch applying their full-court pressure once again, Raptor triggered the ball inbounds to Bird. Waconia's senior point guard dribbled at top speed down the side of the court nearest her team's bench. Just before Bird got to the basket for what would have been a momentum-changing layup, the "pass-first" point guard identified an open teammate. In her effort to pass the ball, Bird lost the handle. The ball slipped from her hands, bounced out of bounds, and went back to Hutch. After 33 minutes of action, 30 of which had been dominated by Waconia, the game was tied and entirely up for grabs.

Hutch had some big post players, but when the chips were down, they relied on their guards to get things done. With important conference and section implications hanging in the balance, the Tigers deployed their dribble-weave offense. It featured four guards outside the three-point line, each dribbling the moment they touched the ball, probing for a seam in the Waconia defense. When the dribbler was prevented from penetrating, she would continue over to the opposite side of the floor, throw a short pass or hand the ball off to a teammate, and the next guard would search for the slightest crack to attack.

After defending valiantly for most of a minute, there was finally a failed defensive rotation by Waconia, leaving a Tiger alone on the baseline. The open Hutch player caught the pass and went for the rim, where she was met by a soaring Raptor.

Predator that she was, Raptor seemed uninterested in blocking the shot. Instead she hammered the Hutch player in a manner that would lead her opponent to reconsider before she dribbled into the lane ever again. Though it took her an extra moment to peel herself from the floor, the Hutchinson player managed to make both free throws and the Tigers had their first lead since the game was two minutes old.

Again Waconia struggled to maintain their composure against the Tigers press. This time a bad Wildcats pass was barely touched by Hutchinson on its way out of bounds. The Cats had dodged a bullet. It would be Waconia's ball under their own basket with 2:20 remaining. Neibs yelled out, "Just get it in!" To the untrained ear, those words made it sound like the coach had abandoned any hope of executing an out-of-bounds play, instead content to settle for a harmless lob to halfcourt that would allow the Cats to set up their offense. That was precisely what Neibs wanted the Tigers to think.

Just Get It In was actually the deliberately misleading name of a Wildcats play. The coach would call out the name loud enough for every player on the opposing team to hear it. Then all four Wildcats were instructed to break out toward the sidelines and the corners of the court. Anticipating a long lob pass that they could steal, the defense would inevitably run with the Wildcats as they spread out, leaving the middle of the lane wide open. That's when Salsa was coached to make her cut. The Tigers took the bait. Salsa cut down the lane untouched and scored a wide-open layup to tie the teams at 60.

A quick drive at the other end resulted in a layup and the Tigers rapidly regained the lead. Hutch swarmed again after their made basket and Waconia's wild pass attempt went out of bounds. This time it had not been touched by Hutch. The Tigers would be given the ball near halfcourt. For the first time since their winning streak had started almost a month before, Dusty could feel the sweat beading above his brow. For a moment, he allowed himself to imagine the flood of angry emails he would have to endure if his Wildcats lost this crucial game after having a late double-digit lead.

The Hutchinson coach, not comfortable protecting a narrow two-point lead, called out a set play. A series of screens by the

Tigers forced the Cats to switch on defense. The switching created the mismatch Hutch had hoped for—5'8" Raptor found herself near the basket defending the Tigers' tallest player. Raptor was surrendering six inches and who knows how many pounds to the big post. The Waconia sophomore invoked all the strength she could muster as the two players fought for position in the paint. As the ball was passed to the Tigers center, Raptor managed to force her much taller opponent into a key miss from a foot away. Raptor then leapt for the rebound and the Cats advanced on offense.

Snake tried a three in front of the Waconia bench. She felt an elbow smash into her face after she let the ball go. Neibs, just a few feet from the play, immediately lobbied the official for a foul to be called. The ref responded that the contact was "inadvertent." Snake's shot missed the mark, but Raptor came to the rescue again. The super sophomore grabbed the rebound and got fouled hard as she attempted a put-back. She missed the shot, but Raptor made both free throws to tie the game at 62.

On the ensuing possession, Hutch hustled down in transition and missed a 15-foot jump shot. In a scrum, Scrunchie snatched up the rebound and started to dribble toward the Waconia end. By the time she bounced the ball a second time, Scrunchie was surrounded by a swarm of Hutch defenders. Scrunchie fell to the ground as the Tigers took the ball away. Not even one second later, Hutch transformed the turnover into two points. The Tigers now had a two-point advantage with fewer than two minutes to play.

Once again overwhelmed by the Hutch full-court pressure, the Wildcats were on their heels. Raptor barely managed to get the ball inbounds to Salsa on the left side of the floor. The long, lanky junior guard drove the baseline, where she was met by the towering Tigers post. Salsa's shot attempt was blocked. There was a mad dash for the ball. Scrunchie chased the ball as it headed out of bounds. She managed to send the ball back onto the court as she went crashing into the crowd, but the ball went in the direction of the wrong team. The instant she caught the ball, a Hutch player promptly fired it across halfcourt, hoping the ball would find a teammate on her way to retrieve it for a layup.

Frantically sprinting step for step with a Tigers guard, Bird managed to win the race to the loose ball by the narrowest of margins. The senior point guard brought the ball back across to the Waconia side of the court, her team still down two after all the chaotic action. Bird passed to Snake on the left wing. Snake took one dribble to her left then attempted to heave the ball back across the floor to Bird. An alert Hutch defender pounced on the pass and held off a hustling Bird. The Hutch player converted the steal into a layup to extending the Tigers' lead to 66–62 with 90 seconds left. A younger player may have pouted about her poor pass, but Snake was never one to dwell on a mistake.

The Cats passed the ball in fast, before the Tigers could set up their press. Fewer than 10 seconds after she committed what could have been the turnover that cost her team the game, Snake cast up a long three-point shot and nailed it to trim the Tigers' lead to one. Dusty took a timeout.

Neibs used the break to remind his team they had time to go for the steal before they would be forced to foul. They discussed defensive matchups and broke the huddle. Neibs was acutely aware of what a loss in this game would mean for his team and for their postseason chances. His heart was hammering inside his rib cage as he reached up to wipe the sweat from his forehead.

Hutch casually passed the ball in while the Wildcats retreated on defense. A moment after the Hutch point guard crossed half-court, Snake struck again. She got a clean steal as the unsuspecting Tigers point guard lifted her eyes to find an open teammate. Snake was racing in for a layup that would put her Cats in the lead. The guard who had been pilfered, desperate to make up for her mistake, caught up just in time to shove Snake as she attempted the layup.

The Wildcats' senior captain hit the floor hard and the crowd gasped. The gym fell silent as Snake lay motionless on the hard-wood. Raptor, Salsa, and Scrunchie ran over to aid their fallen teammate. After seeing she was alert, they helped lift Snake to her feet. Dusty immediately recognized what an important moment it was for his squad. By this stage of the season, Waconia players had been knocked down dozens of times. On each of those occasions, not even once had Neibs seen a group of players rush to lift their teammate from the floor. In the midst of a pulse-pounding finish, Neibs allowed himself a moment to appreciate the way this group of gifted individuals was finally becoming a team.

It took another moment for Snake to shake off the sharp pain that resonated through her thin frame when she walloped the wood floor. Her team trailed by one when she stepped to the line. Snake missed the first free throw. The hundred Tigers fans let out a roar. With time running out and the tension mounting, Snake managed to make the second shot. The score was tied at 66.

The Tigers returned to their deliberate dribble-weave, hoping to wear down the Wildcats defense again. One of the Tigers players appeared to lose her dribble as she was making her way across the court. She had to hastily get her hand high on the ball, which had bounced up near her neck. The Waconia crowd was calling for a "carry," but the ref allowed the unusual-looking dribble, and play continued. Seconds later Hutch attempted a three from the left wing. It hit the back of the rim and Scrunchie skied to grab the rebound in the middle of a crowded lane. She threw an outlet pass to Bird. Bird brought the ball down the right side and swung it to Salsa standing at the top of the arc. Almost immediately Salsa passed to Snake on the left wing. The ball had barely touched her hands before Snake was throwing up another three. The shot missed, but Snake was hammered by a Hutchinson defender on the release. The ref was forced to call another foul. With 32.5 seconds remaining in a critically important game for both teams, Snake would get three chances to break the tie.

Noticeably fatigued, Snake was bent over at the free-throw line, grabbing her knees and gasping for air as she waited for the ref to pass her the ball. Battered, bruised, and breathless, the senior captain courageously made all three free throws and Waconia was up 69–66.

Hutch had to have a three-pointer and they wasted no time, attempting a contested shot from the top of the key. The shot missed the mark and the Tigers grabbed the long rebound near the sideline. The Hutch coach called timeout just before his player lost her balance and fell out of bounds with the ball. The Tigers would get one more chance to tie the score.

During the timeout, Dusty gave the team the same instructions he had while protecting a narrow lead in the team's first win of the season at Hamline. He reminded the team that when they got a rebound or a steal, they didn't need to pass or dribble. The instruction was that they hold on to the ball and let Hutch foul them. The Wildcats would happily shoot free throws and be allowed a chance to set up their defense.

Hutch had the ball in front of their own bench. The play they had drawn up appeared to call for a long pass to the opposite side of the court. Raptor read the eyes of the passer and narrowly missed grabbing a game-ending steal. Instead the Tigers caught the ball and got a wide-open shot at a three. The shot missed, but Hutch grabbed yet another offensive rebound. As they tried to get the ball back outside for one more chance at the game-tying shot, the Tigers were called for a travel. Waconia got the ball back with a three-point lead and 2.2 ticks left on the clock.

Raptor passed in to Snake, and the Wildcats captain was immediately fouled. She went back to the now-familiar free-throw line with 1.7 seconds left. Waconia fans sounded more relieved than excited when Snake made both free throws, securing a 71–66 Wildcats win.

After throwing the errant pass that put Hutch up four, Snake scored nine consecutive points in the final 90 seconds of the game to lead her team to a come-from-behind win. The Brett Favre of Minnesota girls basketball had done it again!

It was a loud Wildcats locker room when Coach Neibauer walked in with the coaching staff. The players were hooting and hollering. After convincing them to quiet down, Neibs reminded the team of his words at halftime. Hutch made their run. The Wildcats responded. Now Waconia found themselves with an important win over a strong section opponent. The Cats were also undefeated in the conference. As he continued his postgame comments, Neibs also acknowledged the moment when the players ran to pick up their fallen teammate. The kids were coming together. They had won seven in a row. The team was heading in the right direction. Neibs closed by saying, "We have to keep it rolling!"

There was no doubt in anyone's mind who "rocked" that night. Snake had put the team on her back in the closing seconds and carried them to a key victory. When Neibs handed over the rock, Snake's teammates let out their loudest cheer of the season.

The gray-and-purple locker room that housed a collection of talented individuals in November was now home to a cohesive, connected group that was genuinely rooting for each other. That is the stuff championship teams are made of.

CHAPTER 9

The Choice

After a full weekend to recover from their hard-fought win over Hutchinson, the Wildcats were reinvigorated as they entered the locker room to prepare for Monday's practice. The dramatic win set up a showdown between the only two undefeated teams remaining in the Wright County Conference. Having graduated a group of important guards, New Prague was not among those projected by the various preseason publications to join Waconia in the hunt for the conference championship. However, as the league season reached its midpoint, the Trojans were 13–5 and in the midst of a long winning streak of their own. With only one day to prepare, the Wildcats recognized they needed to have a great practice.

Her teammates still streaming into the locker room after a full day of school, Scrunchie took a glance through the glass of the coaches' office window to see how the team's fish was faring. She noticed a pink Post-It note stuck to the front of the fish tank. When the girls entered the office to feed their mascot, they were greeted by an encouraging message scrawled on the small square note: "Exciting win over Hutch! Maybe too exciting. My gills were getting goose bumps! Good luck against the Trojans on Tuesday. Thank you for making me a part of your amazing team!" The note was signed simply, "The Fish."

The players had no idea who may have snuck into the locker room to leave the uplifting message, and at that point, it didn't matter. The note had succeeded in putting a smile on the players' faces. They left the locker room in a positive mood and ready for an important practice.

The pace and the execution at practice were the best Neibs had seen all season. The team appeared to finally be dialed in to the message he had been delivering. When the players put their hands together in a huddle at the end of practice, it may have been the first time everyone left the gym feeling good about what they had gotten done.

The next afternoon, as the Wildcats boarded the bus to New Prague, the team felt confident they would take care of business. In a matter of hours, the Cats would be in command of the conference race and on their way to a second consecutive league championship.

New Prague had always been a difficult place for Waconia to play. The town had a reputation for being blue-collar, and in every sport, the school's athletes matched that mentality. The Trojans were never the most talented team, but they would always be one of the toughest, most physical teams Waconia would face. New Prague's school colors were cardinal red and black, but because of the manner in which the Trojans played, the colors opponents most commonly saw as they boarded their bus for home were black and blue.

The focal point of the team's offense for years, New Prague had a big, strong post player. She first played major varsity minutes as an eighth grader. Now, as a senior, she was an absolute force to be reckoned with. Dusty knew that if they could get the Trojans post in foul trouble, the Cats would almost certainly win. With that in mind, the first possession of the game, Neibs called a play designed to get the ball to Scrunchie. The intent was to have the smaller, quicker Scrunchie go right at New Prague's best player. Just as Dusty had drawn it up, the high-scoring sophomore caught the ball on the left wing. Her teammates cleared out to the other side of the court. That was Scrunchie's cue to dribble directly at the New Prague post. As the defender backpedaled, Scrunchie stopped and buried a perfect fadeaway jump shot from six feet out to put the Cats on top 2–0. It was the only lead the Wildcats would have.

Every subsequent second of the 35 minutes of basketball that followed was a disaster. Wildcats passes were thrown to no one in particular. Shots missed the mark by wide margins. Breakdowns on defense allowed the Trojans to take innumerable wide-open shots. Trailing by as many as 24 points in the second half, the game concluded as a 75–56 debacle that left the Cats shell-shocked and gazing up at the underdog Trojans in the conference standings.

After the game, though he was every bit as disappointed as the players, Neibs attempted to dismiss the performance. He pointed out that over the course of a long season, every team will have a bad night. It was simply a bad night to have a bad night.

There was good reason for the coach to do his best to project positivity. Despite the disappointing loss at New Prague, January had otherwise been a banner month for the Wildcats. They had climbed back into the top 10 rankings in Class AAA for the first time since mid-December. The team was well positioned to earn a top-three seed in the section playoffs. A matchup with defending section champion Marshall on February 8 could put the Cats firmly in control of their postseason destiny. Quality time spent together off the court had healed many of the wounds that had opened during the first 10 games. After a turbulent six weeks to start the season, the team's primary goal of getting to the state tournament was well within reach.

Neibs was fond of saying that he was "not a chicken counter," playing off the old adage that one should never count their chickens before they have hatched. While the coach may not have looked ahead at the team's remaining schedule and projected another pile of wins, fans of the Wildcats certainly did. Of the regular season's remaining games, only three were against teams with a winning record. It appeared as though the stars were lining up for the Cats to roll into March with major momentum.

February kicked off with another event hosted by the *Breakdown*. Not to be confused with their season-opening Tip Off Classic, this all-day basketball buffet was called the Community Clash. While it did not necessarily boast a slate of the state's top teams, the appeal was that both the boys and the girls varsity teams from each school were invited, and they would play back-to-back. This offered a rare treat for each town's fans because, with very few exceptions throughout the season, when the girls were playing at home, the boys were on the road and vice versa. Like the girls, the Waconia boys were having a super season, also ranked in the top 10 in AAA. This meant a large contingent of Waconia fans would make the drive to St. Michael–Albertville High School on the first day of February to see both versions of their Wildcats in action.

The girls were excited for the chance to play in front of a group of fans who were not usually able to attend their games. The Cats were also looking forward to getting the bad taste out of their mouth after the train wreck that took place in New Prague. On paper it appeared they would be facing the perfect opponent to resume their winning ways: the St. Louis Park High School Orioles.

St. Louis Park is a suburb of Minneapolis, and the Orioles had struggled to a 7–11 record to that point in the season. With his focus understandably on the team's more recent opponents, Dusty had not devoted as much time to scouting St. Louis Park because, frankly, there wasn't as much at stake. The Hutchinson and New Prague contests had major ramifications for the conference championship and section playoff seeding. St. Louis Park was a nondescript, nonconference game in the middle of a heated conference and section race. Neibs provided the players something of a scouting report, but it was less extensive than most.

The teams battled to a 10–10 tie in the opening minutes, and it didn't take long for Coach Neibauer to get a strong sense this game was going to be tougher than anyone had anticipated. The Orioles had an unusually long, tall lineup. They had three six-footers on the floor most of the time, and one of them was a guard who was being recruited by several Big Ten programs. When the Orioles scored a basket to break the 10-point tie, Neibs began to wonder out loud, "How do these guys have a losing record?"

A few minutes later, the rout was on. The Orioles soared to a 45–25 halftime lead on their way to a stunning 86–58 blowout. One week earlier, the Wildcats were in the midst of a monthlong winning streak. Now, only days later, it felt like everything was falling apart.

As downtrodden as the team was, they had formed a deep and meaningful bond over the past month. A couple bad games would not undo that. No, the players were not about to turn on each other. They were about to turn on Neibs.

The yellow school bus the team rode to and from games was both long and loud enough that conversations could be had in private. The players always huddled in the back few rows of the bus. The coaches congregated in the front two rows, nearest the driver. Only about 12 feet separated the two groups, but the rumble of the diesel engine and the cold wind whistling through the cracks in the windows never allowed a voice to carry farther than a few feet.

As the coaching staff considered what they could have done differently and looked ahead to the next game, the players sat in the back reviewing all the reasons the past two games had been so disastrous. For many people, it is hard to engage in self-examination and accept responsibility when things go wrong. It is infinitely easier to suggest someone else is the problem. The figurative fingers in the back of the bus were all being pointed toward the front of the bus, specifically in the direction of Dusty.

The truth is that from the first days of the season, many of the girls had harbored some hard feelings toward Neibs. They didn't approve of the way he had altered practice from the way it was run under the previous regime. Neibs spent so much time talking and explaining that players were standing around for long portions of practice, and they considered their conditioning to be lacking as a result. Because Dusty divided minutes among 10 players instead of the traditional 7 or 8, none of the players felt they were getting enough time to affect the game the way they thought they could.

Salsa was particularly upset. Yes, the team's top college prospect was embarrassed about losing to a sub-.500 team, but there was more weighing on her mind. Including the game they had just played against the Orioles, Division I college coaches had come to watch Salsa play in person on four occasions. All four times her Wildcats went down in defeat. All four times the game had been so lopsided she had played only marginal minutes and the JV was given "mop-up duty" for a good portion of the second half. Salsa had not scored more than nine points in any of her four opportunities to impress a coach and earn an athletic scholarship. The star junior was worried the team's poor performance on these important occasions could end up being very costly to her and her future.

Adding to the players' angst were the complaints about the coach some of them had been hearing at home. Kids can block that kind of negative commentary out for a while, but eventually it starts to resonate. Comments questioning the competency of a coach can have a far greater tendency to take hold when a talented team loses two games they were expecting to win.

When the team came into the locker room to prepare for Monday's practice, there was another note stuck on the fish tank. This note was longer than what a small Post-It note would allow, so it was scribbled onto a standard-size piece of printer paper, but again the paper was colored pink. It read:

Wildcats,

So I know last week was kinda tough. But this weekend I was thinking back to my days in the ocean and something my good friend Dory used to say.

When the water got rough she'd sing a little song: *"Just keep swimming, just keep swimming."*

If our team just keeps swimming, we are going to get where we want to go. I am proud to be part of this team!

—The Fish

Despite their mascot's best effort, the mood among the players was still sullen. With only one practice to prepare before hosting an important section opponent, the attitudes that emerged from the locker room were decidedly negative. Worthington would likely be one of the bottom seeds in the section playoffs. While it was another game the Wildcats were favored to win, Neibs knew a third consecutive lackluster performance could lead to a loss that would suddenly put his team's postseason chances in peril. With that in mind, Neibs came to Monday's practice with a high level of focus and intensity. The players failed to emulate his approach.

Dusty grew increasingly frustrated as practice unfolded. He reminded the team of what was at stake with the next day's game, but nothing he said or did made a difference. When practice ended, the players made their way to the weight room. Alone in the gym with just his fellow coaches, an exasperated Neibs said, "If we play tomorrow like we practiced today, we're going to have a hard time winning."

The next day, even with the team's trademark sluggish start, it turned out that Dusty's powers of prognostication were not particularly strong. The Cats played very much like they had practiced and were still able to coast to a 79–65 victory. After the game, the fans walked out of the gym with the same understanding the Waconia players and coaches had: Everyone recognized the Wildcats were 30 points better than Worthington, and while it was a win, no one was left with the impression that the team was truly back on track.

The Wildcats had remained uncharacteristically healthy through the first 10 weeks of the season. Other than a few minor ankle sprains and Rookie's bout with pneumonia, no key players had missed more than a game or two. That said, the bumps and bruises were beginning to accumulate, so several players were spending time in the training room before and after practice. Jeff Chrest was the team's certified athletic trainer. A Waconia native, Jeff had been witness to many of the team's trials and tribulations over the years. He had a sarcastic sense of humor that endeared him to the athletes. Though their visits were usually due to injuries, the girls always enjoyed their time in the training room because, much in the manner an older brother might, Jeff would joke and poke fun at the players. The team never took offense because they also knew that Jeff was always looking out for them and doing his best to help them perform at a high level.

Three Wildcats did not have a class the last hour of the day, so they regularly made their way into the training room early. The day after the victory over Worthington, Jeff was attending to some other athletes when the basketball players walked in and started complaining about their coaching staff. Moments later, a few more girls walked in and joined the discussion. Jeff gritted his teeth for a couple minutes, but as the whining went on, the trainer decided he had heard enough. "Get out!" Jeff said. "I've heard enough of the complaining. Go do that stuff in the hallway if you want, but you need to get out of here."

After Jeff's admonition, one of the juniors attempted to explain why Neibs was to blame for the team's troubles. Before she could even complete her sentence, the normally gregarious trainer, in a stern tone said, "You need to respect your coaches. If you're going to talk negatively, you need to leave."

The girls apologized as they exited into the hall. Jeff was still angry at the way they were denigrating Dusty, but he also felt bad for the tone he had taken. He followed them out into the hall and said, "You need to talk to your coaches about how you feel. Complaining to me in the training room won't fix anything. Talk to your coaches."

The practice that followed was not productive. The team was lackadaisical and out of sync. Neibs was not aware of what had transpired in the training room. He attempted to ignite some enthusiasm by modeling it himself. The coach was shouting encouragement and applauding good plays, but nothing he did could turn the practice around. When it ended, Neibs was growing nervous that his team was giving up. The way they practiced and the attitudes they exhibited made it appear they no longer believed they were capable of making it to state. If he couldn't convince them otherwise, the season would be as good as over.

On Mondays and Wednesdays, the team engaged in strength training after practice. The girls had given a good effort in the weight room for most of the season, but on this already dreary day, they drew the ire of Wildcats strength coach Josh Anderson. Josh knew nothing about what had taken place in the training room before practice. He was also unfamiliar with the poor effort they had put forth during practice. That is why it was so striking when, for the first time in his 14 years of working with high school athletes, Josh decided he had to kick kids out of the weight room in the midst of their workout.

After his own attempts to get the girls motivated had fallen flat, Coach Anderson had warned them that if they didn't put forth a better effort, he would end their workout early and it would not be pleasant. With his intern by his side, Coach Anderson stood silently and watched for a few minutes, allowing the players a chance to respond to his warning. When it was clear his attempt at motivation had not worked, the strength coach followed through on his threat. "All right! If you're not gonna work hard in here, then I'm gonna get it out of you one way or another. We're going to the gym!" Coach Anderson hollered.

He announced the girls would run what he called crushers. They would sprint the full length of the floor and back, then immediately run to the far free-throw line and back, halfcourt and back, then finish with a short burst to the near free-throw line and back. "You are going to do this until you figure it out!" he yelled. "Go!"

It took the team 40 seconds to complete the first crusher. After only a few seconds to rest, he bellowed out, "Again!"

After the completion of their sixth consecutive crusher, the players were gasping for air. Their faces displayed the anguish of people experiencing genuine physical pain. Coach Anderson allowed them a moment to catch their breath while he addressed the team. "No leaning over! No pouting! We don't have tired teams here. We have tough teams!" He asked, "You know why you're running, don't you?"

Salsa was only able to muster one word in between breaths. "We're (puff) not (puff) working (puff) hard."

Rookie added, "Our energy is bad."

"You guys are one of the most talented teams to ever come through this school. You've got a chance to do something special. Don't waste the opportunity you have in front of you!" Coach Anderson admonished, before continuing, "Stop with the pouting and the poor attitudes. Work hard and just play the damn game. Now get on the line and let's go again. Go!"

The team struggled through six more crushers before Coach Anderson called them together one more time. "As coaches, we aren't going to let you waste this amazing opportunity you've been given. You have everything you need to do something special. You can do something no group has ever done before. In the few weeks we have left, we need to see nothing but great attitudes and maximum effort. Understood?" So breathless they weren't able to speak, the players managed a nod and they left for the locker room. The only sound Coach Anderson could hear was the players' wheezing as they walked out of the gym.

Not long after the girls had gone home, Neibs went by the training room on the way to his car. Jeff Chrest beckoned Dusty in. The trainer explained the exchange he'd had with the players prior to practice. Dusty had already been informed by Coach Westphal about the unpleasantness that had unfolded in the weight room. Neibs felt the season slipping away. On his drive home, he decided it would be wise to email his athletic director right away so she was up to speed on the team's absolutely awful day.

Jill Johnson was a rarity among athletic directors because she had never been a head coach. She was an accomplished collegiate softball player and had served as an assistant softball coach for a high school team, but she had never directly experienced the day-to-day decisions and pressures confronted by a head coach. That lack of experience did not diminish her ability as an athletic director in the least. Jill was a fantastic advocate for her coaches and as organized and professional as any administrator could be. She would mentor when needed, but Jill never micromanaged her coaches. She was a resource and always available to counsel a coach who was dealing with a difficult situation.

After Neibs's recap of the afternoon's events, Jill shared his disappointment with the direction the team was heading in. In an unprecedented move, she asked if she could address the players before practice the next day.

The Wildcats were about to begin the second half of their conference schedule. That meant they would have a rematch with every team they had faced the first time through. Prior to practice, the girls were scheduled to gather in Dusty's classroom to view video of the next evening's opponent. When they walked into the room, the players were surprised to see the athletic director waiting. As AD Johnson spoke, she reinforced nearly everything the team had heard the day before. She explained that complaining behind a coach's back never cured anything. She reminded the girls how hard Dusty and his coaches were working to get this team to a place it had never been. Jill acknowledged the collection of talent on the team and she implored them to take advantage of the unique opportunity they had during the final weeks of the season.

With an acute understanding of the pivotal nature of the moment for his team and their season, Neibs had prepared four pages worth of bullet points. As Johnson concluded her remarks, Neibs stood up and launched into his own impassioned plea. "We have talked all season about making history, but I didn't think it would be the 'history' of being the first team booted out of the weight room. Our team still has the physical talent to make it to state. What we lack is mental toughness."

For the next ten minutes Neibs addressed the power that each player possessed to affect the attitude of the team. He pointed out that if even one player turns negative, that attitude can spread and infect the rest of the team. The coach made it clear that he would not tolerate players pointing fingers at each other or at coaches when things went wrong. Players were expected to accept responsibility for their actions and their attitudes. "Do you think the best teams in the state behave this way toward each other?" Neibs asked rhetorically. "So let's change our behavior!"

Then the polished public speaker that he was, Neibs shifted to a softer tone to say, "Just imagine what we can be if we simply get over ourselves. If we get out of our own way. Let's see who we can be, unburdened by what we have been."

With his emotions beginning to overwhelm him, the coach was forced to take a long pause in an attempt to collect his composure. He continued, "When we walk out of this room today, we have only two choices. We can continue to undermine and attack each other, failing to live up to our potential, or we start to accept each other loudly, vocally, and accomplish something no group of girls has ever done in the history of Waconia High School."

As Dusty concluded his heartfelt comments, his audience did not applaud. None of the captains spoke up in support of what had just been said. Silently the players left the classroom and walked in the direction of the gym for practice. Neibs knew the season was at a crossroads. With everyone on their way to the gym, Dusty sat alone in his classroom for a moment, wondering which path his players would choose.

Practice provided the coach no clues. While no one would accuse the players of pouting or merely going through the motions, there was no obvious renewed sense of energy or intensity either.

That night in bed, the coach struggled to achieve even his usually inadequate amount of sleep. Dusty interrogated himself in the darkness. *Where did I go wrong? What could I have done differently?* were the most common questions asked by his inner voice. Dusty's expectation of what it would be like to head up his own program had been steamrolled by a harsh reality: Convincing kids to buy into his vision was much harder than he ever anticipated.

Every so often Neibs would glance at his alarm clock with the hope that morning was close enough to justify an escape from the bed that had become his nighttime prison. Unfortunately, the minutes moved slowly. The clock showed it was only 3:15 AM, condemning Dusty to a couple more hours of restless self-reflection. His thoughts shifted to the previous season and the positivity that had prevailed throughout. Neibs silently marveled at the monumental impact one player could have on the chemistry of a team. Last year's lone senior and universally beloved "team mom," Fran, had clearly meant more to the team than statistics had an ability to accurately measure. Fran had been the glue that held the group together. How he wished he could have her back on the team for these final, fateful weeks.

After briefly drifting back to sleep, Neibs's next look at the clock showed 4:40 AM. That meant his forced confinement could finally come to an end in a few more minutes. His inner monologue reverted back to the two choices he presented his players with the day before. What path would they pursue? In evaluating the team's opponent that evening, the coach realized he may have to wait a bit longer before he had the real answer.

Neibs understood the game at Orono that night would not really reveal whether the Wildcats would respond to the pleas of the past two days. The already overmatched Spartans were riddled with injuries. As Neibs expected, Waconia cruised to a 43–20 half-time advantage and waltzed to an easy win. Raptor received the postgame rock for her 24-point, 9-rebound performance. Fellow sophomore Scrunchie added 19 points and 7 boards. A matchup with defending section champion Marshall was waiting with the next sunrise. One more seemingly endless night of tortured, inter-mittent sleep and Neibs would know for certain if the Wildcats' season was over.

Marshall

Every Wildcat wore the blank expression of a poker player as she climbed aboard the bus for the 130-mile drive to Marshall. Dusty was unable to determine what the players' dispassionate eyes signaled. The optimistic view was that they had finally found the focused intensity their coach had been hoping to see all season. Of course, it could also be the look of a team that was counting the days until they could turn in their uniforms.

To Neibs the traditional 12-foot buffer zone of bus seats separating the players from the coaches had never felt further away. The rookie head coach remained unsure if his emotional message had fallen on deaf ears. Had his Wildcats accepted and absorbed all the heartfelt words they had heard from their trainer, their strength coach, and their athletic director? Or had his players decided to merely go through the motions and surrender the remains of what could have been a historic season?

As Neibs waited nervously during the more-than-two-hour drive, anxiety was also the feeling du jour among the players huddled in the back of the bus. The Wildcats were not sure they had what it took to get to state. Like their coach, the players understood that they would know the truth before the night was over.

The Marshall Tigers were a perfect 21–0. They had only shared two common opponents with Waconia. Marshall topped Hutchinson by 10 in the opening game of the season and they blasted New Ulm in much the same manner the Wildcats had.

Waconia walked into Marshall High School with a more modest 15–7 record. Not fooled by their seven losses, Marshall's iconic coach, Dan Westby—already inducted into the Minnesota High School Basketball Hall of Fame—was quick to point out to his players that all seven of the Wildcats' losses came to Class AAAA foes. The veteran coach made sure his kids were prepared for what he was certain would be a very tough game.

The loud, steady hum of the school bus's diesel engine provided a sedative of sorts, allowing most of the Wildcats to get a nice nap during the long drive. When the bus finally made it to Marshall, the decibel level of the engine decreased, rousing the players from their slumber. Sleeping on the drive allowed the girls to enjoy the wonderful illusion that they had only been on the bus for a few minutes rather than the full two and a half hours the drive had actually taken.

Marshall's school colors of orange and black overwhelmed the Wildcats when they walked into the gym. There were bleachers on both sides of the court and six more rows of seating under each basket, similar to the setup at Hopkins. A walking track circled above the court and disappeared into a wall. The track continued into and around the adjacent auxiliary court, where the ninth-grade team would be playing at the same time the JV competed on the main floor prior to the Wildcats' varsity game. A giant, menacing Tiger growled from center court as the varsity players sat down to wait for the JV game to begin.

While most of the team was listening to music and casually watching the preliminary game, Sauce, Rookie, and Salsa reviewed the scouting report one last time. Reading it, they were reminded that Marshall thrived on their full-court trap. The Wildcats should expect to get trapped hard the instant they caught a pass. Defending the pick-and-roll would be important, especially when it featured Marshall's scholarship player. The scouting report made it clear the Cats' top priority on defense was to bottle up the Tigers' best player, No. 14, Jordyn Hilgemann. The last lines of the scouting report were typed in capital letters: "MARSHALL HASN'T BEATEN A GOOD TEAM IN WEEKS. WE HAVE A GREAT CHANCE TO GET A BIG WIN!"

Rookie read the report more intently than anyone else on the team. This game was important to her for personal reasons. Rookie's parents were born and raised in Marshall, and she had been born there too. Rookie was a Tiger until the age of 11. That is when her family moved to Waconia. She had been friends with several of the Marshall players while in elementary school. A fan club of aunts, uncles, cousins, both sides of grandparents, and some other family friends had congregated conspicuously in the Waconia section. Almost all of Rookie's fans had dutifully plucked some purple and gold from their closets to support her and to better blend in with the visitors. The only holdout from the parade of purple and gold was Rookie's 10-year-old cousin; he remained loyal to the Tigers over his own flesh and blood. He couldn't bring himself to abandon his black-and-orange sweatshirt. The fifth grader's only compromise was an agreement to cheer for his cousin but not for her team.

It bothered Rookie that she would be coming off the bench for her big homecoming. She felt a bit embarrassed that all of her relatives and friends would see her sitting at the start of the game. Sure, her parents had explained to everyone that she had been a starter until getting sick, but it still stung. Rookie was committed to showing her fan club that she was worthy of their support. She was also determined to demonstrate to Dusty that she deserved her starting position back.

The person who had taken Rookie's role in the starting lineup had also taken over jump-ball duties at the beginning of each game. Scrunchie stared down the Marshall post as both stood smack-dab in the middle of the mouth of the tiger painted at center court. When the official tossed up the ball, the budding sophomore star was the first off the floor. Scrunchie controlled the tip and directed the ball backward to Bird.

It was an inauspicious start for the Cats, as their second pass of the game was intercepted. With the Marshall player advancing the ball toward her team's goal, Bird turned on the afterburners and attempted to beat the thief to the basket. Though she won the race to the rim, the Wildcats captain wasn't able to get her feet set. Bird was whistled for a foul while the Tigers guard converted the layup. A successful free throw staked Marshall to a 3–0 lead.

The Tigers immediately deployed their devastating full-court press. Waconia was able to navigate through it and execute their half-court offense. After patiently passing the ball from one side of the court to the other not once but twice, Sauce flashed from behind the Marshall defense and was wide-open on the wing. Abracadabra! Sauce conjured some of her famous midrange magic to get the Cats on the board.

Seconds later Snake missed a three and Sauce came crashing in to grab an offensive rebound. She rose up and banked the ball off the board to move her team ahead 4–3. After a Marshall miss, Snake caught a pass at the three-point line. She was fouled as she let an ill-advised three-point shot fly with a defender directly in her face. Somehow the shot went in. Snake's teammates raced over to lift her up so she could shoot the free throw. Snake missed the charity toss, but again Sauce was in the perfect place. The senior collected her third offensive rebound in fewer than three minutes, giving the Cats another opportunity on offense. Sauce's effort eventually set up Scrunchie on the left wing for a long jumper. The sophomore's shot hit nothing but the bottom of the net, and suddenly Waconia was up by six.

As the Cats retreated on defense, Neibs turned to the bench to signal for the first subs to enter the game. Rookie leaned forward in her seat, hoping Neibs would point to her. Instead he called for Mel and Raptor to replace Snake and Sauce. Rookie's face grew red in a mix of anger and embarrassment.

After four minutes of action, Marshall had surged back into the lead. That is when Rookie finally got the call. Her trademark smile was absent as she stepped onto the court. A steely resolve had taken its place. Rookie had something to prove to her family, to her former teammates, to her coach, and to herself.

Confronted with the Tigers' full-court pressure yet again, Ozzie decided to abandon the press break her team had practiced. The speedy backup point guard blew through the sea of black-and-orange jerseys in what seemed like the blink of an eye. Ozzie was still a blur when she arrived at the rim for a layup, but she was moving too fast. Her body had given the ball more momentum than it needed. It banged off the backboard without even touching the rim. Raptor had been running in Ozzie's wake and was right there to get the rebound. Her put-back came up short. Raptor sprung back up to collect her miss. Surrounded by Tigers, she jumped to get above the forest of outstretched arms only to miss again. Scrunchie soared into the scrum to give the Cats another try. Her short shot attempt also missed the mark. Raptor had recovered from her failed attempts to sky over a flat-footed Marshall player and get the Cats' fourth offensive rebound of the possession. This time her two-foot shot fell. Waconia had tied the game at 11.

Marshall's star, the one Coach Neibauer planned to contain, dribbled to the top of the arc and sank a three with 13 minutes left in the first half. Seconds later the ball found its way to Rookie on the right wing and she swished a three to tie the game at 14.

After one more minute of action, Waconia was down 18–14. Snake missed a jumper. Never known as a rebounder, Rookie shoved her way into the lane, fought for the offensive rebound, and was fouled as she tried to muscle it up. Neither of her free-throw attempts even grazed the iron; she swished both to bring her team within two. Now several minutes into the game, the Wildcats appeared to be demonstrating they were every bit as good as the only undefeated team left in Class AAA. That's when the Tigers took over.

For the next six minutes, Marshall outscored Waconia 20–6. The defending section champs had extended their lead to 14 with barely more than four minutes remaining in the first half. The Cats were backed into a corner. After multiple team meetings and all kinds of attempts to inspire, Neibs had been wondering what path his players would choose. He was about to find out.

When Marshall made a turnaround jumper in the lane to extend their lead to 16, most coaches would have taken a timeout in an effort to stop the bleeding. Neibs knew that was what he was supposed to do. Instead, he decided the time had come to test his team and force them to choose their fate.

A wasted offensive possession by Waconia put the Tigers back on the attack. As Marshall moved the ball from one side of the floor to the other, Scrunchie stabbed at a pass with her extra-long arms and poked the ball out toward halfcourt. She sprinted to retrieve the loose ball then proceeded in for an easy layup. Scrunchie's effort not only stopped the Tigers run, it sparked one for Waconia.

After a missed three by Marshall, Snake hauled down the rebound and dribbled up the floor at a furious pace. When she passed to Salsa at the free-throw line, the Tigers defense swarmed. Rookie was left alone on the right wing. Salsa saw the team sniper standing outside the arc and zipped a perfect pass. Rookie tickled the twine from long range to trim the Tigers' lead to 11.

Marshall's next possession ended with an air ball. Scrunchie violated one of basketball's unwritten rules when she lunged to save the ball from going out of bounds under her opponent's basket. Fortunately her desperation heave found Salsa. The Division I prospect displayed her point guard–caliber skills as she maneuvered through the Marshall defenders. When she was finally stopped, Salsa spotted Scrunchie trailing the crowd at the top of the key. Again Salsa passed to the right player. Scrunchie scorched the net to cut further into the Tigers' lead.

With two minutes left in the half, Marshall missed another three-point attempt. Bird chased after the long rebound, catching up to the ball in the corner. The Tigers trapped her immediately, but the veteran point guard was able to dribble around the double-team. Bird got the ball ahead to Snake. Snake snapped a pass to Rookie on the right wing. Marshall would not make the mistake of leaving the sharpshooter open again.

With a Tiger running full speed at her, Rookie recognized the defender's inability to reverse course. She decided to drive the ball toward the baseline. Another Tiger rotated over to stop her, but Rookie used a move worthy of a dancer to deftly sneak by the second defender. Now at the rim, Rookie implemented a finger roll to lay the ball up and in. It was the sixth shot she had attempted in the half and not even one had grazed the orange-painted iron of the rim when going in. Rookie erupted for 10 points in only eight minutes of action, reducing her team's deficit to five as the halftime horn sounded. The Cats trailed 40–35, but they were back in the game and they carried momentum into the locker room. As Rookie jogged off the floor, all the members of her fan club were on their feet, applauding. Even her reluctant 10-year-old cousin couldn't contain his excitement.

Before the coaching staff came in to talk strategy, Will, the fourth senior and the Cats' unofficial player/coach, had some words for her team. "We have a chance! This game is right there for us to take, but we've got to keep rebounding, especially offensively. The second chances we got early are what gave us the lead. We need to get more second shots this half."

Will continued, "When they press us, don't panic. We have proven plenty of times we can break the press. After we get the ball past halfcourt, we just have to slow it down. Be calm."

Neibs didn't convey any major adjustments during the intermission. He spent his time encouraging the girls to go out with the same focus and ferocity they had demonstrated to finish the first half. Neibs sent the team back out for the second half by declaring, "You know as well as I do that we have what it takes to beat this team and win this section. We've got 18 more minutes to prove it to them!"

The second half started with a flurry of fast breaks, fouls, and free throws. Raptor had already been forced to sit for much of the first half with two fouls. She picked up her third foul early in the second half and was banished to the bench again.

With a few minutes gone, the cumulative effect of the Tigers press started to take its toll. Consecutive Wildcats turnovers were transformed into easy layups, and the hosts had built a 50–42 lead. Sensing the game was once again in the balance, Dusty decided to gamble. He sent Raptor to the scorer's table to check back in.

One minute of time had elapsed since Raptor's return. In that brief burst, the Cats had scored once and had already earned the ball back. Mel saw Scrunchie posting up in the paint, so she passed her the ball. With a Marshall defender hanging on her arm, Scrunchie muscled up a shot. The ball barely made it onto the rim. When it finally wobbled in, Waconia trailed by four.

The Tigers missed their next shot and Scrunchie secured the rebound. Demonstrating an ability few posts possess, she pivoted, then proceeded to lead the fast break. Raptor was racing ahead of the retreating Tigers defenders, so Scrunchie launched a long pass in her classmate's direction. Raptor, still running full speed, caught the pass just in front of the backboard. While her momentum carried her body out of bounds, the best athlete on the floor somehow managed to lean back as though she were in a limbo competition and bank the ball in for a layup. The shot was so amazing it made even the most partisan Marshall fans marvel at what they had just witnessed. The Tigers lead was trimmed to two and the Waconia side of the bleachers was bouncing.

A perfectly executed pick-and-roll and a backdoor layup squashed the short-lived Waconia momentum and put Marshall back up by six. Then Raptor scored again in transition, and flirting with her fourth foul, she aggressively jumped in front of a pass and took it to the other end of the floor for a left-handed layup, once again bringing the Cats within two.

A Marshall turnover gave Waconia the ball back. Snake snuck a pass through a triumvirate of Tigers defenders, giving Scrunchie an easy layup to tie the game at 56 with 9:22 to play. A missed shot by Marshall fell to Bird and the point guard brought the ball up the right side of the floor, directly in front of her team's bench. Out of the side of her left eye, Bird saw Salsa filling the fast-break lane in the middle of the floor. She directed the ball to the D-I prospect and Salsa swished a three to give Waconia its first lead since the opening minutes of the game.

Moments later Waconia was still up three when Marshall's veteran coach called a play to get his best player the ball. The Tigers star drove at Scrunchie for one dribble then stepped back and buried a three to tie the game. The home crowd roared its approval when their star player confidently kept her shooting hand up in a gooseneck as she jogged back on defense.

After a big first half, Rookie had not been heard from in the second. When she checked in early in the half, Marshall had made the decision to put their scholarship player on her. As a result, Rookie was having a hard time getting open. When she was able to catch the ball, Marshall's star was instantly in her face. It seemed obvious the message delivered to the Tigers at halftime was to make sure their childhood friend didn't get another open look at the basket.

With just less than five minutes left, the two teams were tied at 61. On most high school courts, there is a volleyball line painted between the three-point arc and the half-court stripe. Waconia had the ball, and as they tried to move the orange sphere from one side of the court to the other, Mel caught a pass standing closer to the volleyball line than the three-point line. To be more specific, she was a full four feet behind the arc, but Neibs's former JV starter did not hesitate. Mel caught the pass, shot the ball in rhythm, and shocked the crowd by making the unusually long three. Waconia was up three with 4:43 remaining.

Raptor had picked up her fourth foul a few minutes earlier. Neibs decided the time had come to go for the win, so he sent his star sophomore back out onto the floor. The move looked like a stroke of genius when Raptor stole a pass on the next play. She had not had the ball for a full second, though, when a little Tigers guard came in and ripped the ball out of her hands, quickly converting her own steal into a layup.

Mel answered back with a quick layup to put the Cats in front 66–63 with exactly four minutes on the clock. On Marshall's next possession, the Tigers tried to pass the ball to the top of the key when Salsa surged, seemingly out of nowhere, to poke the pass in the direction of the Wildcats' basket. Salsa scooped up the ball a step past the half-court stripe and strolled in for an uncontested layup. The Waconia lead was five. Marshall again got the ball to their star, but her three-point shot missed. Mel corralled the rebound, drove the ball up the floor, and found Salsa on the right wing. The lanky guard gave a college-caliber shot fake that sent the Tigers defender flying past her. Salsa then took two dribbles forward before another Marshall defender moved between her and the hoop. Salsa instinctively jump-stopped and shot a perfect pull-up jumper. When the ball came out the bottom of the net, the upstart Wildcats were leading the undefeated Tigers 70–63 with just more than three minutes remaining.

The teams traded free throws for the next 90 seconds. Salsa's two shots from the charity stripe put her team up 73–67 with two minutes to play. In dire need of a score, Marshall was whistled for a travel as they attacked on offense. Waconia was in the driver's seat. They owned the ball and a six-point lead with 1:50 on the clock. However, the travel call had allowed the Tigers to set up their full-court trap. They pressured the inbounds pass, got a quick steal for a layup, and the lead was reduced to four. Marshall applied more full-court pressure after the make. Raptor was able to get the ball in to Bird. The senior point guard was swarmed the second the ball met her hands. A moment later there was a whistle. Marshall started to celebrate, expecting a jump ball to be called. Instead the ref put up his fist to signal a foul. Boos of disapproval rained down from the Marshall fans as Bird toed the line for the bonus. The senior point guard calmly cashed in the first shot, earning a second. The bonus free throw also went in. The Cats were up 75–69 with 90 seconds left.

In an act of desperation, Marshall attacked the lane hard and Waconia was whistled for a foul. It was the 10th Wildcats foul of the half. That meant the Tigers were entitled to two free throws. They made the first and missed the second. Raptor chased after the missed shot, finally catching it in the corner. She was trapped instantly. Instead of taking a timeout, Raptor, with her back to her teammates, tried to throw a no-look pass out of the trap. The ball went out of bounds under the Marshall basket, where it would belong to the Tigers.

As they lined up for their out-of-bounds play, Bird recognized the Tigers' formation from the scouting report. She knew where the first pass would be thrown. Instead of running to deny the pass, Bird waited, baiting the passer into throwing the ball. Then Bird pounced! She stepped in front of the pass, stealing it cleanly. Instead of fouling her, the Marshall players sat stunned. Bird took advantage and advanced the ball across halfcourt. As she had a few minutes before, she saw Salsa streaking down the middle of the floor. This time Salsa continued into the paint, where she received a pass from Bird. By now Marshall had regained their composure and they promptly fouled.

With both teams in the double bonus, Salsa stepped to the line entitled to two shots. Her team was up 75–70 with 80 seconds on the clock. The junior's first shot bounced hard off the back of the rim. With the home crowd heckling her, Salsa's second shot missed long as well. The misses should not have mattered. The Cats only needed to play great defense for one more minute. One more minute of good basketball, and they would send a message to all of Class AAA that *they* would be the team to beat in March.

Waconia fell back as Marshall moved the ball up the floor. Despite stout defense by Snake, the Tigers' star player forced up a desperation three. The shot missed short. The ball caromed hard off the front of the rim and squirted through Salsa's hands. The Tigers star leaned over to grab the loose ball off the ground. When she retrieved it, No. 14 saw a teammate open outside the three-point line and passed it to her. Another Marshall three missed the mark, but the Tigers retrieved the rebound yet again. This time it was the

Marshall post who had the ball. She was positioned conveniently at the block. Scrunchie extended her long arms straight up in an attempt to impede a shot. Scrunchie was incredulous when she was called for a foul. The usually soft-spoken sophomore stepped toward the official with her arms still frozen straight above her head, asking what she could have done differently. The answer, of course, was nothing. The hoops are 10 feet high no matter where you play. The only home-court advantage in basketball is the sub-conscious inclination of officials to please the largest, loudest fan base. So despite her textbook defense, Scrunchie would have to watch Marshall shoot two free throws with 56.9 seconds left.

The Tigers post player made both. Waconia's lead was down to three as Marshall prepared their press again. With no guards able to get open, Scrunchie raced up from halfcourt to offer another option. Raptor rifled the ball into her classmate. One second later, Scrunchie was fouled. Salsa had just missed two free throws that could have extended the lead to seven. The Cats needed Scrunchie to sink at least one of the two pending free throws to make it a two-possession game.

The large Marshall crowd was rattling the bleachers and yelling as loudly as they could to make it difficult for the young Waconia post player. Scrunchie's first free-throw attempt missed to the left. The Tigers faithful were convinced they were the reason for the miss, so they made even more noise as Scrunchie eyed up her second shot. It also missed to the left. The Marshall coach called for a timeout. His team trailed by three with possession of the ball and 47 seconds left.

Out of the timeout, Marshall was handed the ball on the sideline, close to the half-court stripe. They passed in to their star player as she was cutting to the corner. No. 14 then fired a pass to the Tigers post at the top of the key. The post player put the ball on the floor with her left hand and drove down the side of the lane. As she put up a shot, she appeared to be fouled, but the refs put their whistles away. Anticipating a missed shot, an alert Tiger had positioned herself on the opposite side of her driving teammate. With a Wildcat sandwiching her on either side, the Tiger forward jumped up to grab another key offensive rebound and was fouled. Marshall would get two more free throws with 40 ticks on the clock.

Both free throws went through, making the score 75–74 in favor of the Wildcats. After Neibs went to his bench for some subs, Mel was the player designated to pass the ball in against the Marshall press. Again the guards were being denied, so Scrunchie sprinted up the sideline as a safety valve. There was a defender trailing right behind her, so Mel tried to throw the ball away from the defense. Mel succeeded at putting the pass in a place the defender couldn't reach it. Unfortunately for the Cats, it was also too far away for Scrunchie to catch. The ball slipped through Scrunchie's fingers and on to the Tigers bench. Marshall would take possession directly in front of their Hall of Fame coach. The Marshall student section became a madhouse. Neibs was trying to yell directions to his defense, but his voice disappeared into the din.

Marshall elected to implement the same sideline out-of-bounds play they had run only seconds before. The Tigers post player caught the pass at the top of the key and tried to drive down the right side of the lane, but this time Raptor was ready. When the Marshall post put her head down to drive, Raptor held her ground and got run over. It was an offensive foul on the Tigers. The ball would belong to Waconia with a one-point lead and 36 seconds left. To win, all the Wildcats had to do was successfully pass the ball inbounds and make a few free throws after the Tigers fouled.

Marshall again denied the ball to veteran guards Bird and Snake on the inbounds. Mel scanned the floor and spotted Raptor racing toward the rim. Incorporating her soccer skills, Mel reached back and launched a long throw-in type of pass across halfcourt. Raptor caught the perfectly placed ball in stride and headed straight for the hoop. While the pass was in the air, two Marshall defenders recognized what was happening and they converged on Raptor, one on her right and the other on her left. Some coaches would tell their team to slow it down, take time off the clock, and force the defense to foul you. Neibs nearly directed Raptor to do just that, but in the heat of the moment, Dusty trusted his superathletic sophomore to rise above the defense and make what would be a game-clinching layup.

Raptor was coming down the middle of the court directly at the basket. That route to the rim makes a bank shot much more difficult. Raptor rose up and tried to lay the ball just over the rim, but her incredible speed made the ball carry further than she intended. It bounced off the back of the rim and was rebounded by the Tigers. Marshall pushed the ball up the floor as fast as they could. In the chaos of transition, the Wildcats lost track of who they were guarding. Marshall's post player was standing by herself at the block, bouncing up and down in a sort of jumping-jack fashion, desperately trying to attract the attention of her teammate with the ball. A full second later that teammate found her. Snake followed the pass into the paint and bit when the post used a shot-fake. Snake leaped up and landed on the post's shoulders as the shot went up and in. Marshall had trailed by six with 90 seconds left. One minute later they were up one with a free throw coming.

The bonus basket was good and the Tigers led by two with 23 seconds to play. Neibs asked for his last timeout. The plan was to pass the ball in to Snake, have her penetrate the lane and draw defenders. Salsa would stand on the left block. Scrunchie would be positioned on the right. If a defender left one of them in an effort to stop Snake, the senior playmaker would dump a pass off for a game-tying layup. If no help came, Snake would be counted on to finish at the rim and be the hero yet again.

Marshall continued to defend full-court, though they did not deny the guards this time. That allowed the pass to go to Snake as Neibs had planned. She took a moment to examine the defense, then the senior started her attack. She dribbled the ball down the middle of the floor, just as Dusty had drawn up. As Snake penetrated into the lane, Scrunchie was indeed open on the right block; however, Snake fired the pass with such velocity Scrunchie couldn't clasp it. The ball bounced off her hands and out of bounds.

Still trailing by two with only a handful of seconds left, the Cats were forced to foul Marshall as soon as the pass came inbounds. While Waconia had gone a combined 0-for-4 on free throws in the game's final minute, the Tigers post made two more shots to make her a perfect 5-for-5 in the final seconds. Marshall had rallied for a 79–75 win and the Tigers remained undefeated.

Though the final minute of the game was certainly tough to stomach, the postgame mood in the visitors' locker room was not one of disappointment. Just a sophomore, Raptor was the first to speak up. She referenced a website that used a computer algorithm to predict the final score of every high school game in the state. "That dumb website predicted we'd lose by 13, but we all know we could have easily won this game. Sure, it slipped away at the end, but we gotta keep our heads up. We played well. We'll get another shot at them in the section playoffs and we will finish the job." Her teammates nodded in agreement as they applauded her inspiring words.

While Neibs visited with his coaching staff in the hallway, like Raptor, the coach felt that despite the final minute, his team had demonstrated they were serious about getting to state. He decided that during his postgame comments, he would not spend a single second on anything negative. His team had proven to him they had what it took. Dusty's goal was to make sure they believed that about themselves before they left the locker room.

"That was a state tournament–caliber effort, ladies. The way you responded to all kinds of obstacles tonight—trailing by 16 in the first half, players sitting with foul trouble, rallying again in the second half. You had better be as convinced as I am that we have what it takes to get to state."

He continued with his encouraging words: "Raptor, you took that layup late in the game and you missed it, but I want you to know that it was my call for you to take that shot, and I'm betting on you to make it every single time. If you don't make it, that's all right. I put you in that position and I trust you. I want you to take that shot every time. The same goes for Salsa and Scrunchie. You didn't make the free throws, but now you've been in that position and you know how it feels. The next time we get in a game like this you're gonna make 'em. I know you're going to."

He concluded, "Everything had to go wrong for us to lose. The next time we see them, that's not gonna happen because we're not gonna *let* it happen!"

Scrunchie finished the game with 20 points and 10 rebounds and earned the rock. While the team walked out to the bus, Rookie stayed back for a minute to hug all of the members of her fan club. Her million-dollar smile was on display as her family patted her on the back for a great game. Rookie no longer felt ashamed about not starting. It was clear that didn't matter to the people who loved her, so she decided it shouldn't matter to her either.

She was the last player to board the bus, and by the time she did, Rookie felt just like the rest of her teammates. The Cats had proven they were every bit as good as Marshall, if not better. They were committed to making sure they got another chance. When the teams met again, it would be on a neutral floor. After almost a year of wondering if they would ever be able to win the big game, it took a loss to finally convince the Wildcats that they could.

CHAPTER 11

Rock Bottom

Marshall marked the first of three consecutive games where Waconia took on Tigers. Sandwiched in between the Tigers of Marshall and Hutchinson were the far less ferocious Tigers of Delano. That is why when Neibs was informed that Snake would be unavailable just a few hours before tipoff of the Delano game, he did not fret.

Snake hadn't been feeling well during the school day. Her mom managed to schedule a doctor's appointment for 3:00 PM. By 4:00 the Wildcats star had tested positive for influenza A. The doctor insisted she sit out for at least a few days.

The team was as composed as their coach when they heard the news. They knew a win would still be easy to achieve that night, even in Snake's absence. The vacant spot in the starting lineup left Rookie hopeful her recent performance would mean a return to a starting role, if only for one night. She was hurt when Neibs announced Raptor would start in Snake's place.

The Cats made quick work of Delano, cruising to a convincing 64–35 win. Sauce had a stellar game, scoring 8 points and pulling down 10 rebounds. She harbored some hope that her efforts would be recognized with the postgame rock. Sauce had only been awarded the rock just once in the 24 games the team had played to that point in the season. That is why it stung when the honor went to a player who had put up less impressive numbers. Sauce was wounded, but once again she suppressed her pain and frustration. The captain could not create a distraction or a divide. She decided there were more important things than her feelings. Her team was in pursuit of a second consecutive conference championship. There was only one week left in the regular season. A game at Hutchinson and one at home against New Prague were all that remained. Waconia had to win both to claim the conference crown.

With the third of three straight Tigers matchups set for Tuesday, the Wildcats had only Monday's practice to prepare. Neibs spent the weekend watching video of the first time the teams met, the game when Snake saved the day by scoring the final nine points. Watching Snake's last-second heroics was when it started to register with him that due to her illness, Snake would almost certainly be sidelined for the Wildcats' rematch at Hutchinson.

Every school day, Neibs would work "lunch duty." This meant he had to eat his lunch at a table tall enough for him to stand. That vantage point allowed him an angle to scan the cafeteria and snuff out shenanigans. His friend and colleague Drew, a math teacher, was also dutifully positioned at that post each day. In between bites of beef nacho bake or orange chicken, the men would talk about sports or politics. No matter what they discussed, their conversations were always punctuated with plenty of laughter. After a weekend spent wondering how his team would win the rematch with Hutch minus Snake, their senior captain and playmaker, Neibs was not himself, and Drew could tell.

Through the course of their conversation, Drew noticed the notch on Neibs's belt that was most worn out and weathered had been relieved of its duty. Tightened to a new notch, the belt revealed to Drew what Dusty eventually explained: he had lost 19 pounds since November. He had not altered his diet or added additional exercise to his regular regimen. He had surrendered almost 10 percent of his body weight to the stress of the season. With a league title on the line that week and the section tournament starting the week after, the stress would only become amplified. Drew joked that coaching a successful team was the ultimate weight-loss plan. Dusty did not respond with the usual laughter. The best he could muster was a polite smile.

Hutchinson's gym had been recently remodeled and renamed. It was now known as Lindsay Whalen Gymnasium, named for the school's most accomplished alumna. After a standout high school career for the Tigers, Whalen went on to the University of Minnesota, where she led the Gophers to their first and only appearance in the Final Four. The feisty guard was the fourth overall pick of the WNBA Draft, selected by the Connecticut Sun. Whalen was eventually traded to the Minnesota Lynx, where she helped the team win four WNBA championships. Mix in a few

US Olympic gold medals for good measure, and Whalen had certainly built a résumé worthy of having a gym named after her.

The remodel didn't do much to change the main aesthetic of the gym. The ceiling was still so low that if a player attempted a shot from beyond halfcourt, the ball would inevitably collide with one of the even-lower-hanging speakers. There were new black bleachers that spelled out HHS in big gold letters when the bleachers were pulled away from the wall. Seating was still limited to around 800 fans, but having the smallest seating capacity in the conference meant the gym always felt full. The acoustics created by the low ceiling made the 800 fans sound like 8,000 in the closing seconds of a hotly contested game. The most obvious aspect of the remodel were the large digital scoreboards that had been installed at both ends of the gym. With vibrant colors and cool graphics, the new scoreboards were certainly an upgrade over the old-fashioned scoreboards they had replaced.

Hutch came into the game with a 17–7 record, but they had lost the chance to win the conference championship when they suffered a bad loss to Orono two weeks earlier. The Tigers would certainly get some satisfaction with a win, as they could crush the Wildcats' hopes for the conference crown. That said, there was more at stake than simply being a "spoiler." Hutch also competed in the same section as Waconia. Coaches would be voting for playoff seeding at the end of the week. The winner of this game would all but assure themselves a top-four seed and a first-round home game when the section tournament started the following Wednesday.

It wasn't a full house when the game began, but the fans in attendance were loud and rowdy right from the start. The Wildcats gave the home fans plenty to cheer about as the Tigers took a 9–2 lead four minutes into the action. Ten minutes later, Rookie threw in a long three to give the Cats their first lead at 26–24. By the time the first half came to a close, Waconia's lead had grown to five. In the locker room, Neibs let the team know he was proud of the way they were performing, especially in the absence of their senior playmaker.

In the opening minutes of the second half, the Wildcats built on the momentum they had accumulated before the break. A long jumper by Salsa made the Waconia lead swell to nine with eight minutes remaining. Even as the lead grew, Neibs never allowed himself to relax. He knew no lead was safe against the Tigers, especially with the legend of Lindsay Whalen hovering over the home team.

Dusty felt like he was experiencing déjà vu when Hutch tied the game with two minutes to go. Dating back to the previous season, this marked the third-straight matchup when the Tigers had rallied from a big deficit in the final minutes.

Hutch's post grabbed an offensive rebound and scored from a foot away to put the Tigers on top by two with 50 seconds to play. With the Cats' chance at the conference championship on the line, Snake was on the bench in street clothes and unable to carry them to another dramatic last-second win. Someone else would need to step up in her absence.

Still down a deuce with 14 seconds left, Waconia had the ball on the sideline opposite their bench. Rookie triggered the ball inbounds. Salsa, already running toward the rim, caught the ball in stride. She took a single dribble then floated a shot above the outstretched arms of a six-foot-tall Tigers defender. The ball splashed through the net to tie the game at 60. Hutch had the ball last but committed a turnover just as time expired. The teams would need four more minutes to determine a victor.

Mel and Scrunchie were saddled with four fouls. A fifth foul would send them to the bench for the balance of the game. No other Wildcat was in jeopardy of disqualification. Despite that, Neibs neglected to send senior starters Bird or Sauce out to begin the overtime. Ozzie and Rookie joined Salsa, Raptor, and Scrunchie as the Cats hoped to secure a home playoff game and keep their conference championship aspirations alive.

With a little more than a minute left in the overtime, Waconia was ahead 65–64. Then an acrobatic Hutch layup and consecutive Wildcats turnovers propelled the Tigers into a 69–65 lead with 30 seconds to play. A missed shot by Salsa turned into Raptor's 14th rebound of the game. When she bounced off the floor to put the ball in the basket, Raptor scored her 27th and 28th points of the game and brought her team within two. Neibs signaled for a timeout.

Mel was one of the team's best defenders, so she was sent in to replace Rookie. The strategy was to pick up the Tigers in a full-court man-to-man defense. If or when a Hutch player caught the inbounds pass, the Cats would be forced to foul right away. They needed to overplay on the inbounds to force a five-second call or make the Tigers throw a long pass they would have a chance to steal. Famous for their full-court pressure, the Tigers were about to get a taste of their own medicine. For a few seconds, Waconia successfully denied every possible pass. In desperation, the Hutch passer threw the ball long to a teammate streaking toward the Tigers' basket. The low ceiling in Lindsay Whalen Gymnasium meant the long pass had to be a line drive. The passer threw a strike, but it had too much heat for her teammate to handle. The ball bounced off the Hutch player's hands and right into Mel's mitts. The Wildcats had one more chance to tie or take the lead as the clock continued its steady march toward zero.

With precious seconds slipping away, every time a Waconia player caught the ball or tried to drive the lane, a Tigers defender was there to meet her. The ball had made its way to Salsa when the crowd started counting down in unison, "Five, four, three…" When the clock hit two, Salsa was starting to rise up for a fateful shot, but the crowd's count was halted by the tweet of an official's whistle. Hundreds of fans waited in silence, anticipating the all-important signal from the man in stripes. If he threw up a closed fist, Salsa would step to the free-throw line with a chance to send the game to a second overtime.

Instead the referee held up an open hand, signaling a violation. He then proceeded to roll his right and left arms around each other. He called a travel. The unusually low roof on Lindsay Whalen Gymnasium was elevated ever so slightly by the eruption of approval from the home fans.

The Cats' chance at a conference championship had been dashed, but the loss meant even more than that. With five teams in Waconia's section at or near 20 wins and only four getting a first-round home game, the loss definitely damaged the Cats' post-season position. The final game of the regular season would not include a chance at a league championship, but it looked like a must-win if Waconia wanted to argue they deserved a top seed in the section tournament.

The jar of rocks that had been on display all winter, just inside the window of the coaches' office, was sending its intended message. Once filled with 32 stones painted in the team colors, each rock representing a game in the season, all that remained in the now nearly empty jar was a single purple rock perched on a handful that were painted gold. The six gold rocks were reserved for the three section playoff games and for the three rounds of the state tournament. That meant the solitary purple rock symbolized the final game of the regular season. It was against New Prague on Senior Night—the annual evening to honor the soon-to-be-graduates for their years of commitment to the program.

Snake's doctor declared her recovered and gave her the green light to suit up. She would be joined in the starting lineup by Bird and Sauce, and in keeping with tradition, Neibs decided to give Will the first and only varsity start of her career. Scrunchie was the only nonsenior in the starting lineup.

Consistency is usually considered a good quality, but it is not regarded as good when a team consistently starts games slowly. With very few exceptions, all season the Cats had a habit of digging themselves into a hole at the beginning of games. Senior Night was no different. Waconia trailed 8–0 before the refs blew their first whistle. Sticking to the now-familiar script, the team rallied to take a 28–26 lead into the locker room at halftime.

New Prague started the second stanza with a nine to nothing run and built a 35-28 advantage. The Wildcats would claw back to trail 44-43 with four minutes to play, but New Prague outscored Waconia 12–4 to finish. Senior Night and the end of the regular season were punctuated with a disappointing 56–47 loss.

The confidence inspired from the last-second loss (but near-victory) against undefeated Marshall had eroded, washed away by the harsh reality the Wildcats had lost three of their final four games. Neibs was noticeably downtrodden while making his post-game remarks. He conceded the team could end up as low as the No. 5 seed when the coaches cast their ballots the next day. Several of the girls were upset at the idea that section coaches would perceive four other teams as superior to them. Neibs acknowledged he was presenting a "worst-case scenario" and that the Cats could be seeded anywhere from No. 2 to No. 5. However, if the worst case came to pass, Bird, Sauce, Snake, and Will had played on their home court for the final time.

After some sincere comments about the way that she had always put the team above herself and how she was a terrific role model to the younger players, Neibs awarded the postgame rock to Will. As the coaching staff exited, the forgotten fourth senior enjoyed a moment of well-deserved praise and pats on the back from her teammates. With the coaches gone, the mood in the locker room shifted abruptly to one of sadness and frustration.

One of the juniors said to Salsa, "There is no chance we make it to state." A few girls who heard the comment nodded in agreement. Sauce had made it a point to be strong and convey the positive attitude expected of a captain, but she was losing the fight to hide her frustration. On this evening, exactly one year before, Sauce had made a three-pointer at the buzzer to secure a conference championship. But 365 days later, this four-year varsity player felt helpless on the bench as New Prague took the league championship trophy and tarnished what may have been her final home game. Despite her best efforts, Sauce wasn't able to hold back the tears as she left the locker room.

When she got home, through her sobbing, Sauce told her mom, "I don't think we're gonna get to state." Her mom agreed. Sauce also vented her disgust at being inserted into the game for the final 10 seconds, after the outcome had been determined. She said it was "insulting to be put in the game out of pity." Sauce's parents had not offered much of a sympathetic ear all season, but that night, in the most literal way, they became a shoulder for their daughter to cry on.

Sauce wasn't the only Wildcat overwhelmed with emotions. Rookie had also been bottling up her feelings to protect the team. She held it together until she got home. When she walked through the door and saw her parents, she collapsed into their arms and cried. She had suppressed her personal feelings and frustrations for the final half of the season in an effort to help her team reach new heights. Now, having lost the conference crown and facing the prospect of going on the road for an early exit from the playoffs, she felt like her efforts had gone to waste.

Marshall was certain to be the No. 1 seed after finishing the season a perfect 26–0. St. Peter was 20–6. Mankato West had won 19 games. Hutch had a 19–7 record and a recent head-to-head win over 16–10 Waconia. If coaches simply looked at win/loss records, the Wildcats' fate seemed clear. They would return to Lindsay Whalen Gymnasium for their first-round matchup. However, if section coaches considered the grueling slate of games the Wildcats had faced in the first six weeks of the season and the way they nearly won at Marshall, a first-round home game was still within reach.

It was after midnight when Sauce finally settled down enough to climb into bed. As she closed her eyes, she came to the awful conclusion that she likely had only one or two games left in her basketball career. The tears started to pool in her still-closed eyes as she reflected on the huge role basketball had played in her life. The game had introduced her to some of her best friends. It had been the catalyst for her most cherished memories. Basketball had been a bond that connected her entire family. As painful as the past few months had been on a personal level, Sauce was not ready for basketball to end.

CHAPTER 12

Well-Behaved Women

Sauce's dad was cochair of Waconia's famous Nickle Dickle Day three-on-three tournament and a self-confessed basketball junkie. He was also the proprietor of a social media account followed far and wide by fans of Minnesota basketball. It did not surprise him when an equally interested basketball aficionado texted him before dawn with early insight on how the coaches' vote in section two had turned out. What did surprise him is what he was told. In fact, he was so startled he found himself doubting the accuracy of the information. When he received official confirmation at 7:30 AM, he posted the playoff bracket on his social media account.

The stunning news was that the Wildcats were awarded the No. 2 seed. An examination of each coach's publicly posted vote showed Hutchinson had seeded Waconia third, Worthington considered the Cats the fourth seed, but every other team in the section agreed, Waconia was the second-best team behind Marshall.

Shortly after her dad posted the bracket on his social media page, Sauce's phone began to buzz with such consistency it acted as a de facto alarm clock. The flurry of texts was from her teammates, all elated at the news they had been awarded the second seed. The despair that had been the players' predominant mood only hours earlier had been replaced by a euphoric excitement. With the No. 2 seed, the Wildcats felt like they had been given a second chance to salvage their season. That little number next to their name on a bracket had made them believe again.

Later that night, when the stream of text messages finally slowed and the euphoria had diminished, Sauce and her dad drove over to St. Joe's as they had hundreds of times before. The two were alone in the gym—Sauce shooting, her father rebounding for her. For several minutes, the only sound interrupting the faint buzz of the fluorescent lights was the occasional squeak of a shoe on the floor or the swish of the ball through the net. These shooting sessions had historically included light bickering about the arc of Sauce's shot or the placement of her thumb on the ball. On this night there was none of that. There was only a daughter and her very proud father silently reflecting on all the hours they had spent with each other in that gym. On the surface, the sessions had been about getting better at basketball, but in this moment it became clear to both of them that the time together had meant so much more. Finally, as they were about to leave, Sauce's dad broke the silence and acknowledged what both of them had been contemplating, that this visit to St. Joe's gym would likely be their last.

As Sauce started to walk off the court to get her coat, her dad yelled, "Wait!" Sauce turned around to see her father fumbling for his cell phone. "We should record your last shot," he said. Sauce had been winning the battle with the lump in her throat for most of the evening, but when her dad asked that she come back to make one more basket, her eyes were so overwhelmed, a tear finally escaped down her cheek. Obliging her father's final request, Sauce nailed a three-pointer for posterity. Then the dad and his daughter walked out of the gym together for the final time.

With the first playoff game scheduled for Wednesday night, the Wildcats had two practices to prepare for No. 7 seed Mankato East. Neibs had never seen them play, so he spent the weekend emailing coaches he had never met, asking if they would share some video. He was finally able to secure video of one game in late January. Dusty had handled all the scouting himself for the first 26 games of the season, but with the elevated playoff pressure of "win or go home," he decided to enlist a few more eyes. Neibs shared the video with his staff and even asked Waconia's former head coach if he would be willing to offer his analysis. After viewing the video, the former coach's assessment was the same as everyone else's. The first-round matchup with East may be the toughest playoff game for the Wildcats to win. He said, "If you can get past East, you're going to blow out West, and I love your chances of beating Marshall on a neutral floor. But you don't match up well with East. They are scary."

After weighing the observations and input from his advisors, Neibs spent Sunday night putting together a scouting report. He knew how giddy the girls had been after learning they were the second seed. Dusty decided to use the scouting report to set the tone with his team that they were facing a first-round game fraught with peril.

The report started in the usual way, with a look at individual players, their strengths, and what the Cats would try to take away. Dusty discussed the defenses East would employ. Then he closed the scouting report by declaring the Cougars "the most dangerous seven seed I have seen in all of my years of coaching."

Dusty was not necessarily being overly dramatic. Mankato East had concluded the regular season with a record of 12–14, but unlike the Wildcats, the Cougars had momentum heading into the postseason. They had won four of their final six games. Just days earlier, in their final game of the season, East lost by only three to third-seeded Mankato West.

All of the coaches who contributed to the scouting report pointed out how much East resembled the Hutchinson Tigers, and it wasn't only because they shared the school colors of black and gold. East's roster was similar, as they featured an imposing and talented 6'2" post player and a few athletic guards. In fact, the Cougars had beaten Hutchinson 67–58 less than a month earlier. A look at the talent on the team made Neibs wonder how East had ended up with a losing record. Closer examination of the roster revealed a team that did not have a single senior. Their best players were a bunch of sophomores. The young Cougars had learned some hard lessons early in the season, and they appeared to be peaking at the perfect time.

When the Wildcats walked away from the video session at the end of Monday's practice, Ozzie admitted to being "kinda scared."

She was certainly not alone. Neibs had successfully extinguished any overconfidence his team harbored, but he may have taken things too far. The exuberance of receiving the second seed had been sucked away. Fear had filled the void. An excellent motivator for some, fear can have a crippling effect on others. The team would be forced to wrestle with their newfound nerves for another 48 hours.

The thing about East that may have caused the most consternation for the Cats and their coaches was the physically punishing way the Cougars played. For years Waconia players had been told that in the playoffs, the team that pushes and shoves the most prevails. Of course, the Wildcats had always been a bunch of good girls from nice homes who had never had to fight for anything. It was entirely possible that Waconia's biggest problem through all the years of playoff disappointment had never been the officials or their opponents; it was likely their privileged lifestyle. The players' biggest obstacle was the fact they had never really faced any obstacles. When confronted with one, they didn't know what to do.

In the postseason, Waconia was always competing against players from lower socioeconomic situations or from blue-collar rural areas. Put another way, they were competing against kids who had grown up having to fight for everything they got.

Sports are a meritocracy. The Wildcats were in pursuit of something their parents and no amount of privilege could provide. The cost of calling yourself a champion cannot be measured in material things or money. Becoming a champion cannot be bought. But it can be taught.

At playoff time, the Cats' former coach would annually invoke a quote from noted historian and women's rights advocate Laurel Thatcher Ulrich. She famously proclaimed, "Well-behaved women seldom make history."

The coach shared those words in an effort to help his players recognize that getting to their first state tournament, an act of making history, would require the adoption of a different mentality. It would demand a departure from the demure, polite behavior that had been ingrained in the girls their entire lives. The suffragettes who worked for women to gain the right to vote learned that the right would not be given; they had to fight for it. As hard as it was for nice, well-behaved Waconia girls to accept, making history might require being mean.

Neibs attempted to build on this theme as the team's first-round playoff game loomed. When the Cats concluded what could be their final practice of the season, Neibs gathered the girls around and reminded them that they were in pursuit of something historic. "History is rarely given. It is most often taken. We are not going to walk into victory. We will have to rip it from our opponents' arms!"

Neibs knew better than most what would be required, for he'd had a front-row seat to so many past playoff defeats. When other teams were willing to push and shove, scratch and claw (and in the case of Richfield in 2016, quite literally fight with a closed-fist punch to the face), Waconia never fought back. If they were ever to break through, fulfill their potential, and finally earn a place in the state tournament, these young women could not continue to be "well-behaved."

The nerves inspired by the video session and Neibs's scouting report had become amplified on game night as the Cats waited to be turned loose from the locker room. Raptor said, "I've never felt so nervous in my life." The rising sophomore star had merely said out loud what the rest of the Wildcats were feeling.

When the team took to the court for the 20 minutes of warm-up time, the familiarity of their surroundings did something to calm their nerves. They found comfort in the familiar faces throughout the crowd. Seeing their classmates gathered in the student section, covered in purple and gold, gave the girls another boost. With the section semifinals played at a neutral site, Sauce and the other seniors could be certain that no matter the outcome, this would be the final time they competed on their home court. All four of them took some time before the tipoff to scan their surroundings and let the moment seep into their memory.

The next thing that felt familiar to the players was the fact that they found themselves in a quick 4–0 hole. After two minutes East had thrown the ball inside three times and scored twice. Bird got the Cats on the board by making the three in the corner. East scored the next four points, and with four minutes gone in the game, the No. 7 seed had built an 8–3 advantage. Then the Wildcats woke up.

Mel made a three that triggered a 22–3 run by the Wildcats. Offense was not easy to come by for either team, but by half-time Waconia carried a 25–13 lead into the locker room. Neibs applauded the team's obviously outstanding defense, but he opined many missed opportunities on offense. In truth, the Cats' lead should have been at least 20. Dusty's last words before he sent his team out for the second half were meant to motivate: "We need to finish our layups and our other opportunities in the paint in the second half. We need to put this team away!"

Instead of extinguishing the Cougars' hopes, the Cats continued to struggle on offense, allowing East to chip away at the lead. The Cougars had cut the margin to five when Dozer contorted to convert a layup around the much taller opposing post. Bird followed that up with another big three-pointer to build her team's lead back to 10.

With 4:25 left in the game, an acrobatic drive by Ozzie ended with a layup to extend the home team's lead to 48–33. The outcome seemed to be decided. Then, less than a minute later, East had cut into the Wildcats' once-comfortable lead and reduced the margin to eight. Mel answered the Cougars' run with a three-pointer in front of the Waconia bench. Will led the reserves in a choreographed celebration as the lead returned to double digits.

On their next possession, the Cougars scored again, then launched into a desperate full-court press. Like the end of the Marshall game, Raptor received a pass as she was streaking down the floor to beat the press. As she elevated for a layup, she was shoved so hard she flew the full 12 feet from the baseline and collided with the purple pad on the wall behind the basket. In true playoff fashion, no foul was called. East gathered the rebound from Raptor's miss, passed it in to their big post on the other end, and the Cougars' comeback continued.

Again the Cougars employed a press. Snake's defender tried to run right through her to deflect a pass. In the process, Snake was flattened to the ground. This time the refs whistled a foul, so Snake would shoot a one-and-one. She missed the first shot, forfeiting a second free-throw attempt. After another post-up by East's 6'2" powerhouse, the Cats found themselves clinging to a 51–46 lead with 1:24 to play.

With no guards available against the full-court pressure, Scrunchie flashed up as an option for the inbounds pass. She was violently shoved to the ground as she secured the pass in her hands. Her teammates ran over to lift her up. As Scrunchie walked to the other end of the floor to shoot her free throws, her teammates could be heard encouraging her. After the Marshall game, Neibs had told Scrunchie that the next time she was shooting free throws in a pressure situation, he believed she would make both. Now, with their season at stake, the sophomore was in exactly the position her coach had predicted. Scrunchie delivered, making both free throws to increase the lead to seven with just more than a minute remaining.

Waconia held the Cougars scoreless for the rest of the game. Sandwiched in between some free throws, Snake snagged one of her trademark steals and scored a layup to cement the victory. Though they had been pushed and shoved plenty and hadn't yet proven an inclination to push back, the Wildcats had advanced with a 59–46 win.

Surrounded by so many offensive weapons, senior point guard Bird rarely looked to score. She finished the regular season with a modest scoring average of just 2.9 points per game. But with the season on the line and her teammates struggling on offense, Bird had come up big. She was the only Wildcat to score in double figures. The senior point guard's 12 points earned her the first gold rock and propelled Waconia to Saturday's section semifinal.

When the girls gathered in the locker room to prepare for Thursday's practice, they found yellow pieces of paper posted all over the place. Underlined in capital letters at the top, the pages were labeled **THE IMMORTALS**. Below the title were these words:

> For months you have worked, you've sweat, and you've fought,
> Pursuing the prize this team's never got.
> Our teams have tried for near fifty years,
> Every time it has ended in tears.
> But this season will _NOT_ end that way.
> All you have to do is… **_play!_**
> Play as hard as you can, there's no time to rest.
> You are ever so close to being the **BEST!**
> Legends are born from challenge and strife,
> And _you_ can be known for the rest of your life,
> As the team that did it, the team that was **FIRST**,
> The team that _FINALLY_ ended the curse.
> I've heard people say "you can't live forever,"
> It's also been said "you never say never,"
> Do this **TOGETHER** and long after you're gone,
> You'll always be **FIRST**, your legend lives on.

The team appreciated the gesture, but they didn't have time to reflect on the poem that had been mysteriously left in the locker room. They had two practices to prepare for an opponent with 20 wins. There would be time for sentimentality later. It was playoff time. It was time to get to work.

The other three first-round section games went as follows: As expected, No. 1 Marshall mauled New Ulm. In a mild upset, fifth-seeded St. Peter ended No. 4 seed Hutchinson's season. And Mankato West scored 97 points in a blowout win over Worthington and would be Waconia's opponent in the semis. That score got Dusty's attention, as the Cats had only beaten Worthington by 14. Mankato West was a guard-oriented team. They were quick and could score in bunches.

Gustavus Adolphus College was the venue that would host the semifinal round and the section championship game. Located on a hill overlooking St. Peter, Gustavus was founded in 1862 by Swedish immigrants. The college was named after the king of Sweden. From its founding to the present day, Gustavus Adolphus has been closely affiliated with the Lutheran church.

Waconia wouldn't play until 8:00 PM, but the team walked into the gym at 5:30. Ozzie, Rookie, Sauce, and Scrunchie had attended a basketball camp at Gustavus when they were in middle school, but it was the first time in the arena for the rest of the Wildcats. Neibs wanted to give the girls a chance to get acclimated to the surroundings. The Gusties' team colors of black and gold decorated the court. In what could only be called a confusing choice, the bleachers departed from the school colors and were a dark blue. The blue bleachers extended 28 rows high on both sides of the court, so high that the Wildcats' team manager couldn't get a great view of the game even with the team's video camera fully zoomed in. There was a balcony behind one basket. A huge curtain hung behind the other hoop, separating the main court from the rest of the field house. In addition to getting a feel for the arena, Neibs also wanted his team there in time to watch the first half of the other semifinal, which started at 6:00 PM.

While Gustavus was technically a neutral site, top-seeded Marshall had to drive 90 miles while their opponent's drive was barely more than 90 seconds. The St. Peter Saints had the benefit of what amounted to a home game.

The pseudo "home-court advantage" didn't help St. Peter, though. Marshall methodically pulled away from the Saints to win by 20. Neibs and his coaching staff had watched it all, frantically scribbling notes and scratching out plays. The girls only saw some of the first half before they were escorted to their locker room by an official-looking older gentleman with a laminated badge hanging from a lanyard around his neck.

It was immediately apparent Waconia was assigned the least desirable of all the locker rooms. It was so small the girls struggled to get the full team in the room at the same time. Exchanging elbows with an opponent is one thing, but when you are inadvertently clobbering your teammates as you put on your jersey, that is less than ideal. Then there was the heat. Will described the weather in the locker room as "feeling like Florida in the dead of summer." It was both hot and humid. The climate in the cozy room meant the girls would be warmed up before they even took the floor for any pregame preparation.

With their nerves starting to overwhelm them, the players were growing anxious to get on the court. While they waited for a signal that they could exit their sauna of a locker room, Sauce cried out, "We can't lose!" A moment later Raptor declared, "Losing is *not* an option!" Other players started to repeat the phrase. They said it out loud at first, then the words repeated like a mantra in their minds: "Losing is *not* an option."

Most of the players had beads of sweat forming on their faces by the time they left the locker room. Sauce sensed the nervousness of her teammates and offered a suggestion that could help eliminate some of their apprehension. The captain gathered the team in a corner behind the bleachers. "On the count of three, everyone scream as loud as you can," Sauce instructed. Under normal circumstances, her teammates may have rolled their eyes or considered the idea silly. These were not normal circumstances. For almost 10 seconds, the group of high school basketball players let out a primal scream. The blaring pep band kept the sound from circulating through the stands. The Wildcats had released a portion of their nerves into the ether. They felt better and were ready to run out for warm-ups.

As she ran onto the floor, Rookie noticed two things right away. First, the Mankato West Scarlets exuded an intensity and a focus she was not used to seeing. Rookie would usually see smiles and joking from opposing teams when she glanced at the other side of the court during warm-ups. She saw none of that from West. They were all business.

The other thing that was evident was that West had the advantage in the crowd category. Waconia High School had just started its spring break. That meant a good portion of the fan base had made the 30-mile drive east to the airport rather than the one-hour drive south to St. Peter. Mankato was only 13 miles south of St. Peter, so it was almost a home game for the Scarlets.

When the game began, it didn't take long before the Wildcats were reminded that playoff basketball is a different brand. The regular season was called *regular* for a reason. There was nothing pedestrian about the playoffs. The game was not even a minute old when Snake grabbed a steal and threw a long pass ahead to Sauce sprinting down the center of the floor. Snake anticipated the exact moment her teammate would arrive at the rim and the ball got there the same time Sauce did. As Sauce elevated for a layup, a West defender came flying from behind and clubbed her across the arm and head. The ball was knocked loose and Sauce was sent sprawling out of bounds. It was the kind of assault that may have merited an ejection from a college or pro game. But this was a playoff game. The refs put their whistles away and no foul was called.

A different West defender grabbed the ball before it went out of bounds and the Scarlets went on the offensive. Sauce scraped herself off the hardwood and hustled back into the paint just in time to stand in the path of a guard driving directly for the rim. Sauce stood her ground and took a charge, and this time the official had no choice but to blow his whistle. Twice in the span of 10 seconds, Sauce had been sent to the floor. It was a sign of things to come.

Three and a half minutes into the game, Waconia players had hit the deck a half dozen times. Some of the shoves were called fouls, some were not. But during that same span, nary a West player had been pushed, much less sent to the ground. *Well-behaved women seldom make history.*

Seconds later Raptor was racing in for a transition layup when she became the latest victim of a Scarlets attack. After four minutes of having herself and her team beaten up, Raptor was in a rage. The most physically imposing player on the Waconia roster was about to send a message that the Scarlets would receive loud and clear.

On the next offensive possession, Raptor caught the ball halfway between the right wing and the corner. The sophomore took two hard dribbles and never even bothered to look at the rim. Raptor lowered her shoulder and ran over her defender with the ferocity of a fullback plowing into a pile of linemen. The West defender was knocked clean off her feet, flying backward onto her butt. It was the first time a Scarlet had hit the floor. Raptor gave a defiant glare as the ref called a charge. It was clear she didn't care. She just needed to even the score. *Well-behaved women seldom make history.*

After all the years Waconia had been beaten up in the playoffs, it was a sophomore who finally found the will to fight back. From that moment on, the Wildcats' attitude was altered. Raptor had proven it was OK to push, it was all right to fight. And for the rest of the game, that is precisely what the Wildcats did. They trailed 8–7 at the time of Raptor's intentional offensive foul. Waconia outscored the Scarlets 24–10 after the collision and built a 31–18 lead by the half. The Cats continued to scratch, claw, and fight for the balance of the game, increasing the lead to as large as 24 points.

Raptor poured in 21 points, Salsa added 12, and Scrunchie posted 11 points and 10 rebounds in the win. Marshall had stuck around to scout for the section championship game. Neibs knew the Tigers players were going to be dealing with nerves of their own after witnessing his Wildcats and their newfound ferocity.

CHAPTER 13

All of Us

They had been in Neibs's backpack for a full year. He brought them out to show the team in November and on a couple of occasions during the season when he thought the girls were losing sight of the ultimate goal. The last time he had taken them out of his bag was right before the loss at Marshall. Dusty was debating whether or not he should pull them out one final time before the section championship.

They were the runner-up medal from the previous season's loss in the section championship and the net he'd had the players practice cutting down the day before the Cooper game. The JV coach at the time, Neibs had been insistent that the last task on the practice plan the day before the section final had to be making each player climb the ladder to cut down a net so they would know what it felt like to celebrate a state tournament trip.

"Our players have never done it. They have never seen it done. They don't know how it feels to win. We need to practice it!" Dusty demanded. The head coach capitulated. Though they considered it hokey, the girls reluctantly did as they were told. A ladder was lifted from the custodian's office, and with Dusty doing his best to simulate crowd noise, each player climbed up to practice cutting down a portion of the net. Having come seconds away from engaging in the ceremony last March, Dusty was determined that his team would do it for real this time.

The runner-up medal awarded by the MSHSL was festooned with a red ribbon. Blue ribbons belonged to the champions. Throughout the season when Neibs felt like his team was losing focus, he would sometimes shout, "Do you want to be stuck with a red ribbon again this year? I'm all about getting that blue!" After almost four months of working, sweating, and struggling, the Wildcats found themselves in the position they hoped to be in: 36 minutes away from making history.

With spring break in full swing, the Wildcats didn't have to wait until the end of the school day to practice, so Neibs scheduled Monday's practice for 10:00 AM. The championship game would be on Thursday night. Given how Waconia had played in the semifinals, the coach would have preferred his team play sooner rather than later to maintain their momentum. Further, Neibs knew the reputation of Marshall's Hall of Fame coach, Dan Westby. Dusty feared that three days to prepare would prove to be more of an advantage for the Tigers than for his team.

When Dusty distributed the scouting report on Monday morning, he had made minimal adjustments to the game plan from the first time the teams matched up. He expected Marshall would again press and trap aggressively. The undefeated Tigers had forced the Cats into 27 turnovers in the first game, so he was certain the Tigers would trap hard again. Dusty changed up the team's defense on the pick-and-roll and included a new out-of-bounds play. Then the coach closed the scouting report with what he felt were the two most important phrases. He considered them so important he typed them entirely in bold letters:

"It will take all of us."

"Greatness will not be given. We must rip it from their hands!"

The Cats had three great days of practice. The team finally demonstrated the kind of focus Neibs had been hoping to see all season long. *Better late than never*, he thought.

After Wednesday's practice, the girls gathered at Snake's house for a team dinner, just as they had done before the semifinal game. The aforementioned legendary basketball coach Don Meyer left dozens of deep thoughts for future generations. Among them was the suggestion that there are two ways to build a team. One is through shared suffering. The other is through shared experiences. Throughout the season, these Wildcats had engaged in both. The team had been tested by tribulations, many of their own making, and they had invested time in each other off the court to cultivate a deeper bond. Once a collection of talented individuals segregated by grade, the Cats had melded into one team with a common goal.

At 7:00 that evening, the girls gathered in the Waconia High School gym again, this time to cheer on the Wildcats boys in their first-round playoff matchup. With so much of the student body gone on spring break, the girls and boys basketball teams had made a pact to support each other through the playoffs. The boys had made plenty of noise in the girls' win over Mankato West. The girls were excited to return the favor. Neibs didn't discourage them from attending the game, but he did remind his players not to stay up too late, as they had an important game of their own the next day. The girls' enthusiastic support helped propel the boys to a 10-point win and their own section semifinal.

The Wildcats endured one more night filled with more restless anticipation than sleep, then the big day finally arrived. The bus would leave for St. Peter at 3:40, but Dusty wanted the girls to come in for one more mental walk-through and to put up a few shots before they left. From 2:45 until 3:30 the Cats reviewed their opponent's plays and practiced a few of their own. They shot some threes and some free throws. When the time came to gather their gear and get on the bus, Sauce lingered in the gym for an extra minute. As her teammates walked out, she caught herself gazing up at the girls basketball banner displayed on the wall behind the main basket. There was no shortage of conference championships on there, but the bottom half of the banner—the area reserved to acknowledge state tournament appearances—was utterly empty. This game would be Sauce's last chance to leave her mark on the bottom half of that banner.

On the drive, the players were not nearly as nervous as they had been before the previous game. The way they had dismantled the Scarlets gave them a kind of confidence they hadn't felt all season. With the girls in good spirits, the most nervous person on the bus was Neibs. He was contemplating the added impor-tance of the game given that Waconia's window in Class AAA was almost certainly closing in the near future. Then chatting with his staff, Neibs noted that amidst all the relief they had felt in the spring with the announcement of a move to a new section, the Wildcats' remarkably unfortunate streak of having the state's best team in their section remained intact. There were only three teams in all of Minnesota that had not yet suffered a loss: Class AAAA powerhouse Hopkins, Class AA Pelican Rapids, and Waconia's opponent that evening; Marshall was a perfect 27–0.

As the team stepped off the bus at Gustavus, they were greeted by the same elderly gentleman who had been their escort for the semifinals. Much to the girls' chagrin, he showed them to the same small sauna of a locker room they had dealt with a few nights before. Ever the optimist, Rookie grinned and declared it "good luck." The girls decided to agree.

Continuing with the superstitions, Sauce encouraged her squad to engage in another pregame primal scream. They converged in the same corner they had before the semifinal and let out another collective yell. When the Wildcats emerged from behind the bleachers, their spirits were lifted by the vast sea of purple in the stands. Despite spring break siphoning off some of their fan base, a look at both sides of the bleachers suggested the Wildcats would be playing what amounted to a home game.

Of the Waconia residents who had not escaped to warmer climes, many of them had made the 60-mile drive to St. Peter. Among the purple-clad fans were two former Waconia coaches.

Mark Pudlitzke guided the girls to the region championship game in 1989, and Tom Doyscher led the Wildcats for 15 seasons and had experienced his share of near-misses. Both men may have felt compelled to attend that night with the hope that witnessing a Wildcats win may exorcise the proverbial demons and afford them some measure of mental relief. The two retired coaches were there as representatives of the hundreds of girls who had grown into women, still haunted by what might have been.

The current coaching staff never talked to the team about the "curse," but they didn't have to. Even if the present-day players were not aware of all the depressing details from decades past, they had each been witness to more recent heartbreaks, watching from the stands as elementary and middle school kids.

When this year's Wildcats walked onto the court for the section final, they carried the weight of 45 seasons worth of coming up short with them. Generations of young women had come agonizingly close to the prize that was now within their grasp.

With the pep band belting out the 1986 anthem "The Final Countdown" by Europe, Waconia peeled off their warm-up shirts to reveal their white road uniforms with purple piping. Undefeated defending section champion Marshall looked intimidating in black uniforms with orange trim.

As the official stepped into the center circle, Dusty took a deep breath and contemplated the moment. After coming seconds away one year earlier and clawing their way back to the section championship game, Waconia was on the precipice of achieving their goal. After a months-long roller-coaster ride of a season, the Wildcats found themselves just minutes away from making history.

When Scrunchie controlled the opening toss and sent it to Snake, the Waconia fans cheered loudly as though the opening possession was worth a point. The Tigers defense started in a 2-3 zone. The Wildcats cautiously passed the ball back and forth around the perimeter for several seconds. Then Salsa caught the ball on the left wing, suckered the closing defender with a shot-fake, took one dribble inside the arc, and drained a long jumper. Waconia fans elevated their arms in unison. Some were waving purple pom-poms. There was only the occasional gold accent in an otherwise massive wave of purple.

Three minutes later, the game was tied at four. A whistle for a jump ball gave the Wildcats possession on the sideline opposite the Marshall bench. Snake cut into the near corner, where Bird passed her the ball. Raptor set a screen for Salsa on the far side of the floor. When Raptor's defender followed Salsa for a fraction of a second, the sophomore saw an open lane and cut to the basket. Snake fired a strike to her cutting teammate. As Raptor rose up for an easy layup, her defender raced back in an effort to correct her mistake. She fouled Raptor as the ball was bouncing off the glass and through the net. Raptor missed the free-throw attempt she had earned by being fouled, but Scrunchie skied for the rebound and scored a put-back. Again, the Waconia faithful roared their approval.

On the Wildcats' next possession, Raptor caught the ball on the left wing and somehow managed to get from the three-point line to a left-handed layup in a single dribble. The lead was now 10–4 in favor of Waconia with exactly four minutes expired in the first half.

Marshall responded with a three-point play. The Wildcats went back on the attack. Salsa showed off her dribbling skills and sliced down the lane. Just as three Tigers defenders converged on her, Salsa saw Raptor alone in the right corner. Salsa zipped the ball out to her open teammate. With both feet behind the college three-point line, Raptor threw in a three-pointer to extend the lead back to six.

Raptor scored the next four points for Waconia before getting a brief break on the bench. While she rested, the Wildcats failed to score. Right after Raptor was reinserted into the game, she drove the left baseline and was fouled. The sophomore forward made the first free throw and missed the second; for the first 10 minutes, Raptor was basically beating the Tigers by herself. With 7:30 left in the first half, the score was 17–12 with Waconia in the lead.

Two minutes later, Ozzie grabbed a rebound and went coast-to-coast for a layup, extending the Waconia lead to nine. The student section, anchored by the entire boys basketball team, could not contain their excitement. Marshall was forced to take a timeout.

Neibs used the timeout to adjust his team's press break. Marshall was not trapping the first pass as they had in the game a month before. They were playing a much more passive full-court zone. It was a blessing for the Wildcats, but Dusty expected Marshall would start amping up their defensive pressure soon. The coach was doing his best to get his team mentally prepared.

The stoppage in play succeeded in squelching some of the Wildcats' momentum, however the guys in stripes were the ones who brought any remaining momentum to a screeching halt. Mel, Dani, and the red-hot Raptor were all whistled for their second foul in the span of just 60 seconds. The subsequent parade of Tigers to the free-throw line allowed Marshall to trim the Waconia lead to two.

With Marshall gaining momentum, Bird delivered the ball to Rookie a step behind the college three-point line. The junior drained a long three to stop the Tigers' run and push the Wildcats' lead back to five. As Marshall came back on offense, Scrunchie channeled Boston Celtics legend Bill Russell when she blocked a Tigers shot and grabbed the rebound before the ball hit the ground. Scrunchie threw an outlet pass to Bird. Bird advanced the ball to Rookie on the right wing. Recognizing the Marshall defender would come flying out at her, Rookie used a shot-fake. With her defender stuck in midair and unable to adjust, Rookie drove into the lane, where she was fouled by a different defender. The sharpshooter swished both free throws. Rookie's personal 5–0 scoring run had, at least for the moment, thwarted her hometown's comeback. The Cats were back in control at 26–19. Marshall took another timeout.

Waconia was leading 29–25 with 1:13 left in the first half when Ozzie buried a big three to increase the lead to seven. One minute later, Sauce leapt into a passing lane for a steal. She passed ahead and hit Snake in stride for a layup. Marshall's last-second shot circled around the rim and fell out. Waconia was up 34–25 at intermission.

In an impressive demonstration of the team's depth, 25 of the Cats' 34 first-half points came from players who began the game on the bench. Raptor had 13, Rookie and Ozzie were responsible for 5 apiece, and undersized post Dozer added a deuce. As Neibs had proclaimed in the scouting report, "It will take *all* of us."

While they couldn't complain about the score, all was not well for the Wildcats as they walked into their hot, humid locker room. Scrunchie and Salsa had picked up their second fouls late in the first half, joining Mel, Raptor, and Dozer. That totaled 5 of the team's 10 varsity players in some degree of foul trouble. The game was not being officiated like a traditional playoff game. The Cats would have to adjust.

Neibs addressed that and some other strategic concepts at halftime. He closed his comments by saying "We are 16 minutes away. Let's go make history. Let's go to state!" The Wildcats came sprinting onto the court, excited for the second half to begin.

It was Marshall's ball to begin the half. The Tigers started by missing an open jump shot. Sauce grabbed the rebound and passed to Snake. The senior guard attacked in transition, driving down the lane and drawing defenders. Snake saw Sauce running in the lane to her left and dished to her. Eight feet out on the baseline and alone, Sauce conjured some midrange magic and the lead grew to 11.

For the next several minutes, Marshall was never able to narrow the lead to fewer than nine. Then Marshall made a move. The Tigers' star player drove the left baseline and was fouled as she made a layup. After making her free throw, the Waconia lead was

reduced to seven. Both teams followed with a few empty possessions. The length of time without a basket led to a growing feeling
in the arena that the next team to score would have the upper hand.
Snake sensed the gravity of the moment. The playmaker stepped in
front of a Tigers pass and went end to end for a layup, moving the
margin back to nine.

With 8:41 remaining, Scrunchie was fighting for position
in the post when, in an obvious attempt to fool the official into
calling a foul, the Marshall player defending her flopped to the
floor. The acting job was convincing enough for the ref to whistle
Scrunchie for her fourth foul, forcing the Cats' top rebounder and
second-leading scorer to the bench. Marshall got the ball back and
took advantage of Scrunchie's absence by cutting the Wildcats'
lead back down to seven.

On the ensuing possession, Waconia patiently passed the ball
around, taking almost a full minute off the clock. To everyone's
surprise and despite their deficit, Marshall was still not pressuring
on defense. After a few more passes, Snake caught the ball in the
corner. The gunslinger of Minnesota high school basketball was
getting bored. She had seen enough passing. Snake fired up a high,
arcing three. When she released it, Neibs could be heard saying,
"No, no, no," but when the ball banked off the glass and through
the basket, the coach yelled, "Yes!" The lead ballooned back to 10.

With five minutes remaining, Mel grabbed a steal and threw a
long pass ahead to Raptor. The sophomore soared with a layup to
make the score 57–46 in favor of the Cats. Immediately after the
shot, fists were pumping and purple pom-poms were waving all

throughout the Waconia side of the stands. The fans were becoming convinced that 45 years of heartbreak were about to come to an end.

The Wildcats' lead was still 11 when Scrunchie was fouled with 41 seconds left. As Scrunchie walked to the free-throw line, she and Raptor shot each other a look. As Raptor's face grew into a big grin, Scrunchie could feel tears welling up in her eyes. Best friends since second grade, no words needed to be exchanged. Both girls knew exactly what the other was thinking. It was happening. Their dream was coming true.

Simultaneously the Wildcats bench was coming to the same conclusion. The game was over. Sauce turned to Ozzie and screamed, "We did it!" As the senior captain leaned over to give her teammate a hug, Rookie scolded her and said, "Don't jinx it!"

Struggling to see clearly through her tears, Scrunchie missed her free throw, but Marshall missed their next shot so badly it went out of bounds. The Tigers took a timeout with 30 seconds left. When the Wildcats gathered at the bench, Neibs was still strategizing. The pep band was playing, so Dusty had to shout his instructions. "I don't want a turnover! Get the ball across halfcourt and kill the clock!"

Neibs glanced up from his white board to see Snake and Bird giggling. The girls were laughing because their coach had not yet accepted the obvious. They had done it! They were going to state!

When the final buzzer blared and the bench players rushed onto the floor, everyone wearing a Waconia jersey was locked in a giant embrace. Tears flowed down the cheeks of smiling faces and fans hugged each other in the stands.

Bird (No. 2) was bubbly and charismatic off the court but a tenacious competitor on it. Will, the senior who accepted a reserve role, is smiling on the right. TIM KRUSE

Unsure whether she would even play, Mel made a big impact in several key games.
TIM KRUSE

The JV players sat on the varsity bench and brought this kind of energy to every game.
ROXANNE KUERSCHNER

Salsa elevated her play when the Wildcats needed it most: the playoffs.
ROXANNE KUERSCHNER

The ultimate playmaker, Snake lofts one of her trademark running one-handed jumpers. ROXANNE KUERSCHNER

Sophomore sensations Raptor and Scrunchie share a celebratory moment after the section championship. ROXANNE KUERSCHNER

Backup point guard Ozzie overcame ACL surgery and the fear she would never be the same.
ROXANNE KUERSCHNER

Coach Neibauer (Neibs) took a lot of heat during his first year as a head coach but never lost focus on the goal.
ROXANNE KUERSCHNER

Raptor soars for a score at the Barn, the University of Minnesota's historic Williams Arena. ROXANNE KUERSCHNER

Sophomore post Scrunchie won a spot in the starting lineup midseason and finished the season as the Wildcats' second-leading scorer. ROXANNE KUERSCHNER

Rookie (No. 21) was relegated to a reserve role midseason but continued to hit clutch shots off the bench. ROXANNE KUERSCHNER

Snake triumphantly cuts down her portion of the net after the section championship game. ROXANNE KUERSCHNER

Backup post Dozer was a defensive specialist who provided a physical presence. ROXANNE KUERSCHNER

Snake soars for a layup after yet another steal. ROXANNE KUERSCHNER

Sauce hid from her teammates how much she was hurting in an effort to be the consummate captain. ROXANNE KUERSCHNER

Sauce (No. 5), Coach Neibauer, and the rest of the Wildcats enjoy the adulation of the large contingent of Waconia fans after the section final. JAMES STITT, *WACONIA PATRIOT*

After a few minutes of spontaneous celebration, the Wildcats lined up to shake hands with the previously unbeaten Tigers. In the moment they passed by each other, Snake felt bad for her opponents. She flashed back to how she had felt at this time one year earlier. The senior was grateful she did not have to experience that anguish again.

The handshakes complete, both teams lined up for the awards ceremony. The Tigers received the medals with the red ribbons and their runner-up trophy, then the Wildcats had the coveted blue ribbons hung around their necks by their athletic director. Three weeks earlier, athletic director Jill Johnson had begged the team to take advantage of this very opportunity.

Next came the moment Neibs had forced them to prepare for. Though it took a year longer to execute than he anticipated, each player finally took her turn climbing the ladder to cut off her commemorative portion of the net. Neibs was the last one up the ladder. He cut the remaining loops, then thrust the net high over his head. A giant grin completely consumed his face. After a team photo with the medals and championship trophy prominently displayed, the team retreated to the walk-in closet they called a locker room. While Dusty was being interviewed by multiple media outlets, the team had some time together, out of public view, to bask in their historic achievement. Shortly after arriving in the locker room, the players turned on their cell phones to find an emotional video message from the leader of the previous year's team. A freshman on the St. Cloud State women's basketball team, Fran was not able to attend the game, but she had listened intently to every second of the radio broadcast online. In the video, Fran was crying as she conveyed how proud she was of her former teammates.

"I know what an awful feeling you all experienced last year," Fran said. "I'm so happy you made it to state this year!"

Raptor wanted to make sure their "team mom" had a chance to share in the moment. She used FaceTime on her iPhone to bring the former captain into the postgame locker room. The entire team was crying and laughing as they relived the game with the leader who had inspired them so much the season before.

As the call with Fran came to a close, Rookie shouted out an idea: "When Neibs comes in, we need to pour water on him!" A teammate naively asked, "Why?" Rookie responded, "Because that's what players do to a coach when they win the championship!" It was decided the seniors would be the ones to execute the ice-water assassination. Will, Snake, Bird, and Sauce quickly removed the lids and held water bottles in both hands. The captains waited just to the side of the door. One second after Neibs walked in, the seniors hoisted the bottles above their heads and sent a waterfall cascading down on their coach. While most of the freezing water found its intended target, there was some collateral damage. Coach Westphal had been following directly behind Dusty and she also received an unexpected shower. The shock of ice-cold water was not enough to wipe the smile off either coach's face.

It had been almost an hour since the Wildcats cemented their names into the Waconia High School history books. Neibs knew he needed to keep his postgame comments short. "I told you all year that it would take all of us. We had five players in foul trouble tonight, and we counted on players who didn't always get a ton of time. You stepped up!" The players cheered and clapped.

Dusty continued, "Tonight we kept our turnovers low. We played great defense. We finished in the paint. We handled their press. We did all the things we knew we needed to do. But more important than all of those things, we came together as a team!"

There was no doubt in anyone's mind who deserved the post-game rock that night. Raptor made 9 of her 10 shot attempts, scored 22 points, and had played terrific defense on the Tigers' top player. The group huddled together one more time and Neibs yelled out "Team on one! One!" In unison, the players responded loudly, "Team!"

"One team!" was what the Wildcats had shouted for years when they broke the huddle, but this group, through all their struggles and setbacks, had truly become the embodiment of those words. So many players had put their personal goals aside and surrendered themselves to the team. A key varsity player for three seasons, Sauce had accepted a reduced role. Will worked for years to be a role player on the varsity. When she was denied that chance, she didn't walk away or attempt to divide the team. She found other ways to contribute and always put the team first. Rookie rode a roller coaster, beginning the season as a starter before being asked to return to a reserve role. Such a demotion would have caused some kids to quit. Rookie cared too much about her teammates to consider such a thing. Even the player who ended up leading the team in scoring for the season, Raptor, started only two games all year. Not once did Raptor whine or complain. Some scored or played more than others, but every player had a significant role in securing the section championship. Everyone on the Wildcats sacrificed something. They and their teammates overcame the selfish impulses that suffocate so many talented teams. This group had finally lived up to its mantra. These Wildcats were absolutely and forever united as *one team.*

CHAPTER 14

Immortals

Waconia would have to wait until Saturday to discover who they would face in the first round of the Class AAA state tournament. While seven of the eight section champions had been crowned on Thursday night, there was one final in the southeast corner of the state that wouldn't take place until Friday. Saturday morning, the head coach from each of the eight champions would speak on a conference call about where they felt their team should be seeded and why.

The Minnesota State High School League started to seed all of the state tournaments in 2007. In that inaugural year, the coaches voted and teams were assigned their seeds based on the vote. The following year the format changed because a soccer team complained that being labeled as the No. 8 seed hurt their players' feelings and "ruined their season." In an effort to placate the patsies, the league decided to seed No. 1 through No. 5 based on the coaches' vote, then randomly draw the other three teams and assign them an opponent.

Though Waconia had the fewest number of wins of any team in the field, Coach Neibauer made a strong case that his Wildcats were worthy of a top-three seed. Boasting a schedule loaded with the best teams in Class AAAA, the Wildcats lost to a Class AAA school only once all season. Then they avenged that lone loss when they toppled the only undefeated team in the entire class.

Waconia was the only team in the field of eight that had never been to a state tournament. In fact, five of the other seven teams had been to state on a semi-regular basis over the years. The seven other coaches didn't seem to care about what the Wildcats had done to get there. As the new kids on the block, the Wildcats were not voted one of the top five seeds. The random draw put Waconia in what would have equated to the No. 6 seed. That meant they would face the 26–2 Red Wing Wingers in the opening round.

Dusty was disappointed his team wasn't shown more respect by the other coaches. He was also upset when he saw where his team's first-round game would be played. With 32 teams from four different classes converging on the University of Minnesota campus, it was impossible to fit all of the games into the premier venue, Williams Arena. As a result, some of the first-round games were played in the adjacent Maturi Pavilion. The Pav, as it was called, was the home court of the Gophers volleyball team. It seated about half as many people as the cavernous arena the Gophers basketball teams called home. Opened in the early 1990s, the Pav also lacked the history and ambiance of the Barn, the affectionate nickname Gophers fans had given to Williams Arena.

As a senior in high school, Neibs had come one game away from playing in Williams when his Fertile-Beltrami Falcons fell in the first round of the state tournament. While he was grateful he had guided the Wildcats to their first state appearance, Dusty was still one win away from achieving the goal he had clung to since he was 18 years old. If he wanted to walk onto the historic court at Williams Arena, his Wildcats would have to win one more game.

When school resumed on Monday, everyone at Waconia High School was excited for the girls basketball team. Walking the halls, the players felt like celebrities. In between classes and at lunch, they were showered with congratulations and compliments. The team's first game was at 4:00 PM on Wednesday. With the announcement students could be dismissed from school early to attend, classmates who hadn't come to a game all season were suddenly jumping on the bandwagon. During class, each teacher took a moment to applaud the girls' historic accomplishment. The players were still two days away from their first state tournament game, and already the experience had surpassed any of their expectations.

A pep rally was planned for Tuesday at 10:00 AM. That is when all 1,200 students at Waconia High School would gather together in the gym to give the girls an enthusiastic send-off. Replete with a pep band, the energy in the gym was palpable. When the Wildcats were introduced, they were showered with applause so robust it was audible over the blare of the band belting out the school song.

Athletic director Jill Johnson acted as the master of ceremonies. She reminded the crowd of the historic nature of what they would witness the next day. A Waconia girls basketball team would be playing in the state tournament for the first time ever. Then she encouraged students to purchase their tickets in advance at the activities office so they could avoid the long lines at the arena. At that point, the microphone was handed to Coach Neibauer.

After saying the obligatory thank-yous to all of the ancillary people involved with the program, Dusty introduced the team. The coach began by calling out each player's nickname. Only as the crowd was applauding did he mumble the player's actual, legally given name. The four seniors garnered the most enthusiastic response from the crowd. Again, speech teacher that he was, Neibs knew his way around a microphone. He launched into an extemporaneous recap of the season and the team's accomplishments. Then the coach built to a crescendo and closed with a line he had been reciting to the team regularly: "You don't walk into history. You rip it from the arms of anyone that stands in your way!" The crowd of more than 1,000 students cheered the coach's fiery and heartfelt conclusion.

The pep rally ended with AD Johnson encouraging students to circle the basketball court so they could high-five the team. The players formed a line and took a victory lap around the floor, soaking in the adulation of their peers as the pep band again played the school song.

Observing the pep rally along the baseline of the basketball court was the lead high school sports reporter for the state's largest newspaper, the *Minneapolis Star Tribune*. David LaVaque's articles were read by Minnesota sports fans from those nestled next to the Canadian border in International Falls all the way south to Albert

Lea along the Iowa state line, and by everyone in the 400 miles in between. When LaVaque asked to interview Snake and Raptor after the pep rally, the girls began to fully understand what a big deal it was to reach the state tournament.

Not long after the interview, it was time for the team to board the bus for their send-off tour. The black-and-gold bus was escorted by police cars and fire trucks as it pulled out of the high school parking lot. The brigade of lights and sirens led the team to the middle school, then to each elementary school, where students were lined up on the sidewalks to cheer and wave as their heroes made their way to Minneapolis.

The next morning, the *Star Tribune* article featuring Waconia appeared at every gas station and grocery store across the state. When Minnesotans grabbed the paper off their front porch, the headline at the top of the sports page said, DEVASTATING SEASON ENDING LOSS FUELS FIRST STATE TOURNEY TRIP FOR WACONIA.

The story began with a brief recap of how the Wildcats had come so close the season before only to have their hearts broken. Then Snake, who had certainly cemented her place as one of the greatest players in Waconia history, was asked about the previous season's loss in the section final. Her response was profound. "We were all just devastated because we were one basket away," she said. "Coming back this year, we knew we had to get to the other side."

The senior captain had encapsulated it with exceptional clarity. After her team had come so agonizingly close, they were able to anticipate the elation; Cooper's last-second shot had sentenced

Snake and her teammates to a year imprisoned on the wrong side of glory.

This incarnation of the Wildcats was able to break free from the shackles of past failures, shackles that had confined all the teams that came before them. They had successfully escaped to the other side, and it was glorious indeed.

With the fanfare literally in their rearview mirror, the team's attention turned to their first-round opponent, Red Wing. The Wingers were not newcomers to the state's biggest stage. This was their fourth state tournament appearance in the past 10 years. Red Wing had a particularly impressive season, losing only twice. The Wingers had not simply been winning; they had been dominating, beating every opponent by more than 20 points for the final month, including an eye-popping 30-point win in their section championship game.

The previous summer, the Wingers and the Wildcats had faced off at a tournament in St. Cloud. Summer games sometimes feel more like a scrimmage, and they certainly fall short of the intensity seen at the state tournament. That said, the only time the teams had met, Red Wing absolutely had their way, beating Waconia by 20. Dusty wasn't discouraged by the experience. He remembered well what Red Wing had done to dismantle his team. The coach was confident he would have his Wildcats ready for the rematch.

When the Cats came onto the court for pregame warm-ups, Raptor was in awe of the atmosphere. The Maturi Pavilion was nearly packed, and both student sections were already on their feet, competing to see which could make the most noise. The sophomore had never seen so many students at a game. It gave all of the Waconia girls a great lift to feel the support of their classmates and their community.

As the lower seed, the Wildcats were again wearing their white uniforms with purple-and-gold trim. Contrary to what one would expect given the name of the town, Red Wing's primary school colors were purple and white. When Scrunchie and her opposite number converged at the massive maroon-and-gold *M* at center court, both student sections were jumping up and down in unison, shaking the lower level of the stands as though there was an earthquake.

The Wingers won the tip and Scrunchie was called for a quick foul. Red Wing got on the scoreboard first with a free throw. On Waconia's first possession, Sauce set a high screen for Salsa near the middle of the court. The smooth junior guard glided to her left and swished a jumper just beyond the free-throw line. Waconia's fans went crazy.

The Cats led 7–3 when Scrunchie was whistled for her second foul. The game wasn't even four minutes old and Waconia's best rebounder and second-leading scorer had been banished to the bench. Neibs reminded the team "It's gonna take *all* of us" as Dozer checked in for Scrunchie.

Neibs knew Red Wing's offense was predicated on back doors and basket cuts. He had drilled his players to anticipate the cuts during the three practices they had in advance of the game. As the game progressed, it was becoming increasingly obvious the Wildcats' diligent preparation had paid off.

Moments after she subbed in, Dozer stepped in front of a pass to the post for a clean steal. She threw a quick outlet to Ozzie. The lightning-fast point guard immediately passed the ball up the sideline. The ball found Mel with her feet so far behind the three-point arc she was almost out of bounds. Long-range was the distance Mel seemed to prefer. She let the ball fly without a moment's hesitation and it snapped through the net to put the Wildcats on top 13–4.

Red Wing rallied to cut the Cats' lead to one with four minutes remaining in the first half. With the momentum shifting, Dusty decided to gamble. He sent Scrunchie and her two fouls to the scorer's table. Waconia was up 20–16 with 1:55 left when the sophomore center was whistled for her third foul. That put Scrunchie and the Wildcats in a precarious position for the rest of the game. Again Dusty turned to his team and reminded them, "It's going to take *all* of us!"

With the clock winding down, Snake attempted one of her patented pickpockets as the Wingers point guard crossed halfcourt. The official was of the opinion no player's hands could legally move so fast. He signaled Snake for a foul. Red Wing made the first free throw and the bonus shot to again reduce their deficit to one with 21 ticks left on the clock.

Dusty called for his Cats to take the final shot of the half. With six seconds left, Sauce had the ball and a wide-open look at the basket. She waved her midrange-magic wand, and—abracadabra!—the Wildcats were up three as the horn sounded to signal the end of the first half.

The University of Minnesota volleyball team was very protective of their locker room, so both Red Wing and Waconia were relegated to storage rooms while they made their halftime adjustments. Each makeshift locker room was adorned with folding chairs and a rolling dry-erase board. Dusty conferred with his coaching staff in the concourse while fans filed past with their refreshments. When Neibs walked in, the first thing he said to his team was, "We've got to stop jumping at shot-fakes. That's why we have a couple of people in foul trouble. Keep your feet. Make them shoot over you."

Neibs continued, "We also need to get the ball inside."

Scrunchie interrupted, "We can't do anything against Deming [Red Wing's center]. She's the strongest post we've ever gone against."

"That may be, but we can't just bomb threes all game. Draw her up into the high post and attack her with the dribble," Dusty replied. "We can't change who we are based on the opponent. We gotta double down on who we are, do the things that got us here in the first place," he concluded. "Get in here. Team on one. One!" And the players shouted, "Team!"

Nearly three minutes into the second half, Red Wing's All-State sharpshooter got free for a three to give the Wingers their first lead since the opening minute of the game. Down 24–22, Neibs turned to the bench to get five fresh players. Ozzie, Mel, Raptor, Rookie, and Dozer would be expected to win back the lead. Two minutes later, the Cats trailed 24–23 when Dozer dove and snagged another steal. From her knees, she maneuvered a pass to Ozzie. Ozzie fired the ball far up the sideline to Rookie. Positioned right in front of the Waconia bench as she caught the ball, Rookie's teammates started to stand, raising their arms up to signal a made three-pointer before the blonde bomber had even let go of the ball. Rookie made her teammates look like fortune-tellers, splashing the ball through the net and reclaiming the lead for her Wildcats.

With nine minutes left in the game, Red Wing had the lead back and the ball. Snake tipped a pass. Scrunchie snatched it out of the air and beat the Wingers to the basket for a layup. Waconia was back on top 30–29.

As the low score would suggest, every possession had been a battle. Both teams were playing smothering defense. Points were at a premium. On the very rare occasion a player was able to get an open shot at the basket, the iron had not been kind.

Three full minutes passed without a score by either team, then with six minutes left, Red Wing regained the lead at 31–30. Neibs responded by calling a play designed to get his best shooter the ball. Rookie delivered from downtown again, draining a three from the top of the key to give the Cats a 33–31 lead.

As the fouls mounted for both teams, free throws became more common. Maybe it was the deafening noise of the crowd. Maybe it was the larger arena. Whatever the reason, even at the free-throw line, both teams struggled to get the ball to go through the net.

With three minutes to play, it was a free throw that put the Wingers back in front 34–33. Her Wildcats in need of a basket, Bird brought the ball across the center line and instinctively passed to the player who had made more clutch shots than any Wildcat in history. Snake caught the ball on the left wing. She drove toward the baseline. When it became apparent she wouldn't make it to the rim, Snake pulled up off one leg and lofted a shot. A Winger collided with her at the apex of her jump, but by that time the ball was already on its way through the basket. Waconia claimed the latest advantage in what had become a back-and-forth affair.

Red Wing's powerful post responded with a drive of her own to propel the Wingers in front with 2:20 to play. Seconds later a turnover by Salsa gave the ball back to Red Wing.

The Wingers spread the floor and were clearly trying to kill the clock. They had the Wildcats right where they wanted them. Red Wing ran an offense designed to exploit opponents that were overly aggressive. Down by one and with no shot clock, Waconia was forced to overplay the passing lanes. The higher-seeded Wingers had successfully subtracted 20 seconds from the clock when Snake stepped in to save the day. The senior playmaker snuck up behind a Wingers dribbler and plucked the ball away as it bounced back up off the floor. As she advanced in the other direction, Snake found herself engulfed by Wingers defenders. Out of the corner of her eye, Snake saw a white jersey streaking to her right. She threw a pass not knowing for sure who the blur of white was. Salsa came into view just in time to catch the no-look pass and convert the layup. Waconia was up 37–36.

After 35 minutes of trying, on one of their final offensive possessions, Red Wing finally got free on a backdoor cut. Salsa sprinted into the lane just in time to commit a foul that prevented an easy layup. With 39 seconds left, Red Wing's forward missed the first free throw. The Waconia fans were ecstatic. The Wingers' second free throw went through and the Red Wing side of the pavilion erupted. The score was tied.

Dusty took a timeout and diagrammed a play for Salsa. As they had done all game, Red Wing defended the play well and Salsa's shot missed so badly it went out of bounds. Red Wing would get one more opportunity to win the game with 15 seconds left. With the clock approaching zero, one of the Wingers had the ball on the right side of the floor. She started a drive toward the baseline when suddenly the ball bounced off her foot and trickled out of bounds as time expired.

Waconia's first state tournament experience would be extended for at least four more minutes. The teams headed to overtime.

Scrunchie had fouled out with 3:30 left in regulation, so the five on the floor to start the extra session were Snake, Bird, Salsa, Raptor, and Dozer. During the regular season, Sauce had gotten upset when she was left on the bench late in close games. Now those feelings of frustration were far removed from her mind. Sauce was not the least bit concerned about her personal playing time. She was completely invested in the success of her team.

Red Wing won the overtime tip but missed a midrange shot to open the extra period. Raptor secured the rebound. During the break after regulation, Dusty repeated his direction from halftime. The Cats complied and passed the ball inside the paint to Dozer. Her missed shot resulted in a tie-up. A jump ball was called, giving Waconia possession under their own basket. For only the second time all season, Neibs called out the trick play Just Get It In. After all the Cats cut hard toward the corners, Raptor knifed into the lane for an easy layup. The Wildcats had struck first.

Considering how anemic their offense had been for the first 36 minutes, it didn't take long for Red Wing to respond with a bucket of their own. When Waconia got the ball back, they patiently passed it around for most of a minute. Then Salsa caught a pass at the top of the arc and had enough room to launch a long three. It was a bull's-eye. The Wildcats were up 42–39.

Red Wing attacked the lane on their next possession and Snake swatted the shot attempt out of bounds. To the crowd it looked like a clean block, but the official had seen a foul. The Wingers made both free throws. Not content with a one-point lead, Dusty dialed up another play for Salsa. When the Wingers prevented the play from developing, Snake decided it was time to make something happen. The Brett Favre of Minnesota basketball elected to drive down the lane. Dusty held his breath. When the defense collapsed to stop her, Snake zipped a perfect pass to Dozer standing alone at the right block. The backup post paused for a fraction of a second, then a rush of adrenaline flooded her veins, causing her to shoot the ball with too much force. The crowd of thousands was quiet with anticipation watching the ball bounce hard off the backboard then rattle around the rim. Finally the ball fell through the net and the Wildcats' lead was back to three with 1:24 to play.

Red Wing needed to score on the next possession to keep hope alive. As they got into their offense, Raptor recognized what the Wingers' next move would be. The emerging young star exploded into the passing lane and stole the ball. Raptor got the ball to Salsa before Red Wing could foul. The junior covered the ball up with both arms, allowing the defenders to hit her. Salsa wanted to be the one at the line to put the game out of reach.

With the Red Wing crowd doing their best to distract her, Salsa swished both free throws to extend the advantage to five with 63 seconds left. Raptor attempted another steal as Red Wing attacked the rim, but she was found guilty of a foul. The Wingers made both free throws to make the margin one possession. However, in the final 50 seconds, Bird and Salsa were perfect at the free-throw line to secure a 52–45 upset victory. In their first trip to the state tournament, the Wildcats were advancing to the Final Four.

Dusty's admonition that it would "take all of us" turned out to be true. All 10 players who had stepped on the court for the Wildcats scored. While everyone had contributed, there was no debate about who had earned the gold rock. Salsa was the star of the game, tallying 19 points, 9 of them in overtime. As they jogged off the Pavilion floor, the girls were greeted by throngs of students handing out high-fives.

As Will described it, the Wildcats were on "cloud nine" as they made the 15-minute bus ride from the University of Minnesota to their hotel in Falcon Heights. Walking into the lobby, the team was again confronted with the magnitude of making a state tournament. A large Waconia Wildcats logo was on display on all the TVs in and around the front desk.

The four senior captains were assigned to a room together, and before they had a chance to catch their breath, the glitz and glamour that came with competing in a state tournament was put on hold. The underclassmen came to the captains' room with their sweaty game-worn uniforms. The seniors were charged with the task of washing them in the bathtub of their hotel room so they would be clean and ready for the semifinal game the next day.

By the time the team went out to dinner that night, the talk had shifted from the exhilaration of a state tournament win to a discussion of world events. Something called coronavirus had been dominating the news cycle for the previous 24 hours, and events were unfolding fast. The day before the state tournament started, there had been talk that the NCAA basketball tournaments might be played in empty arenas. When the team's food came out of the kitchen, the news broke that the NBA was suspending its season.

Immediately the players began to wonder what that major development would mean for them and the continuation of their state tournament. Neibs didn't have any answers yet. He tried to encourage the kids to enjoy the moment, but it was clear the virus had already infiltrated the team's thoughts. Exhausted from an emotional day, the girls didn't have to be told to get to bed at a decent hour. All of them were asleep in their hotel rooms by 10:00. Neibs and his coaches had no such luxury. They were up late formulating a game plan for their semifinal opponent, the Becker Bulldogs.

The No. 2 seed, Becker had lost in the state championship game the year before. Like Red Wing, they had only been beaten twice all season. The Bulldogs lost to the soon-to-be-named national champion Hopkins Royals 77–39 at the Tip Off Classic in November. It was hard to hold that loss against them. Their only other defeat came at the hands of Hutchinson. In late December, the Tigers toppled Becker by 10. That gave Dusty and the Wildcats confidence they could match up favorably with the state tournament–seasoned Bulldogs.

The Wildcats were scheduled to play at 2:00 PM, so Dusty decided the opportune time for the girls to eat breakfast would be 10:00 AM. The bus drove the Cats to a pancake house. After their meal, the team traveled directly to historic Williams Arena.

Home to the Big Ten's Minnesota Golden Gophers, the building opened in 1928 and had changed relatively little in the century since. Though it was referred to as the Barn, it was far from cold and drafty on game nights. When the Gophers hosted a Big Ten rival, the arena was almost always filled to its 15,000-seat capacity. Hanging high in the rafters were the retired numbers of legendary players Dusty had heard about as a boy. There were a few he had the pleasure of seeing play, though only as NBA stars. Mychal Thompson of the Los Angeles Lakers (father of NBA star Klay Thompson), former New York Knick and Chicago Bull Trent Tucker, and of course Boston Celtic and NBA Hall of Famer Kevin McHale. The retired numbers of the women's basketball legends hung on the other end of the arena. Dusty took an extra moment to appreciate the banner representing current Gophers head coach Lindsay Whalen.

Neibs knew when he stepped up from the bench onto the famous elevated floor that he was standing on the same sideline where coaching giants such as Tom Izzo, Bo Ryan, and Bobby

Knight once walked. With his players trailing behind him, the coach paused, turned back, and said, "Hey, look around. Take it in. Look where you've made it. This is the dream."

To the casual observer, it appeared he was talking to his team, but it may well have been that Dusty was speaking out loud to the 18-year-old version of himself, the part of him that had longed to compete on this hallowed ground since the day he was denied the chance in Fertile-Beltrami's first-round state tournament defeat. Nearly two decades later, his dream had become a reality.

Not long after they arrived at the arena, Dusty's athletic director intercepted him and asked him to come with her. When they had moved out of sight of the team, Jill Johnson told Neibs she had some important news to share. "We just received word from the State High School League that Saturday's state championship games will be played without fans. The actions being taken by the pro and college leagues have really forced the MSHSL to follow suit," Johnson said.

Dusty was disappointed. The idea of a championship game in an empty arena was not the way anyone wanted it to be. AD Johnson continued, "Also, the third-place games have already been canceled. So the team that loses today, their season is over."

As dejected as the news left Dusty, he was reluctant to share it with his team before tipoff. He debated the best course of action in his head for a few minutes, then dutifully determined the girls had a right to know what was at stake before they stepped on the court. It was not yet halftime of the other semifinal game when Neibs broke the news. The team took it harder than he expected.

Salsa described herself as "devastated." Raptor was weeping. While all the players were affected, the news hit the seniors the hardest. A first-round win at the state tournament was supposed to guarantee the girls at least two more games before their career came to a close. A public health crisis had put the Cats in a win-or-go-home scenario. The team had about an hour for the situation to sink in before going out to play the biggest game of their lives.

The players' mood was lifted considerably when they were escorted to their quarters. They would be in the locker room that belonged to the Gophers men's basketball team. They weren't allowed to bring in their phones, but one of the coaches snuck her cell past security and got some cool pictures and video of the fancy facility that she would share with the squad later.

Another exciting thing about reaching the semifinals was having the games broadcast on TV across the state. Because of the broadcast, the pregame introductions always took a little longer, as they included the reserve players for both teams. It was a chance for Will and the rest of the JV squad to wave to the camera and get a few seconds of fame before the starting lineups were announced.

When the game began, most of the lower bowl of the Barn was occupied. Ozzie confessed that the combination of thousands of fans and being on statewide TV had her stomach in knots. She must not have been the only nervous player. The two teams combined to miss the first nine shots of the game. A couple of those shots included air balls. Finally, two and a half minutes into the action, Scrunchie drove and drew a foul. She made both free throws and the Wildcats were in the lead. Becker missed the first shot of their next possession, but an offensive rebound afforded them a second opportunity. The Bulldogs turned their second chance into a three-pointer.

Bucking conventional wisdom that it was harder to pressure full-court on a longer college floor, the Bulldogs decided to give it a try. Waconia had seen their share of full-court pressure throughout the season, but they hadn't encountered a team like Becker. The Bulldogs featured five fast guards, a couple of whom had long arms, making passing more perilous. The Cats were having a hard time getting open against the Becker pressure.

With less than a second to spare, Snake snuck the ball past a diving defender and safely into Bird. The senior point guard broke through the press and found Raptor posting up in the paint. The sophomore forward turned around and got a fadeaway jumper to fall. Waconia was up 4–3. It was the last lead the Wildcats would have.

After five minutes of ice-cold shooting, the Bulldogs didn't just get hot; they became as scalding as the surface of the sun. By halftime Becker was more than halfway to 100 points, building a 54–34 lead. Waconia was shell-shocked as they retreated to the locker room.

While the coaches conversed outside in the hallway, the mood among the players on the other side of the door was decidedly negative. Scowls and growls abounded. Then Sauce spoke up and said, "This is supposed to be fun!" The other seniors echoed her sentiment. Rookie added, "We are at the state tournament. We have so much to be proud of." There was talk of mounting a comeback, and everyone agreed they would absolutely do their best to get back in the game. However, the group also resolved to make the best of whatever time they had left. The mood had shifted by the time the team climbed onto the court to warm up for the second half. The scowls had been replaced by smiles.

Halftime had done nothing to cool the hot shooting by Becker. Waconia was able to trade baskets with the Bulldogs for most of the second half, but they could never cut significantly into the lead. Trailing by 21 with five minutes remaining, Dusty was trying to determine the best time to sub out his seniors. Neibs wanted to make sure the JV kids got a chance to play on the famous floor, getting their moment in the television spotlight, but he also wanted to be respectful to his captains.

Bird and Snake were already in the game. With 4:19 remaining, Neibs called for Sauce and Will to replace Raptor and Scrunchie. The Waconia crowd applauded loudly for the subs. After first joining forces in fifth grade, the final time the four seniors would play together was on the state's biggest stage.

At this point, the team's primary goal was to get the ball to Will. The forgotten fourth senior would make the memory of a lifetime if she could manage to score a basket at Williams Arena. Neibs called out the same play for Will that had gotten Rookie free for a couple of big three-pointers the day before, but the Bulldogs snuffed it out. The next offensive possession, the play called for Will to set a back pick, then open up to the ball for a three. The scrappy senior set such a good screen, Sauce was wide-open for a layup, so Snake delivered the ball to Sauce for the easy deuce.

Next, Snake got a steal and passed to a streaking Salsa for another layup. After a foul sent Becker to the free-throw line with 2:11 left, Neibs decided it was time to give the JV their chance. The four seniors walked off the floor to thunderous applause from the Waconia faithful. The captains were crying as they stepped down off the elevated floor to take a seat on the bench. A decade worth of basketball memories came flooding back as their careers officially came to a close.

When the final horn sounded, the Wildcats had fallen 96–75. It was an emotional postgame locker room. The feelings swung from sadness that the season had ended to pride at what they had overcome and ultimately accomplished. Neibs thanked the four seniors for all they had contributed to the program. He applauded how far they had come as players but also how much they had grown as people. The challenges they had faced and the lessons they had learned would make them better coworkers, better bosses, better spouses, and better parents. Finally, the coach emphasized this group of girls would always share a bond by being *first*. First in the history of Waconia High School to reach the state tournament.

Sauce finished the game a perfect 5-for-5 from the floor. A smile parted the stream of tears rolling down her cheeks when she was awarded the final rock of the season.

By halftime of the Wildcats' game, fans' phones were informing them that the NCAA had completely canceled March Madness. It wouldn't be announced until the next morning, but the Minnesota State High School League would be forced to cancel the rest of the girls' state tournament as well as the boys' tournament scheduled for the following week. Because of a virus that would soon be called COVID-19, 2020 would be a year without a champion.

The Wildcats were blissfully unaware of what the MSHSL would be announcing when they boarded the bus for home. At that point, the team's top priority was getting back in time to cheer on the Waconia boys in their section championship game at 7:00 PM. The boys team had been tremendously supportive, even making it to Williams Arena for the game that afternoon. The girls wanted to be there for what would end up being the boys' final game of the season.

When the bus pulled into the Waconia High School parking lot, some of the players went directly to their cars and headed home so they could get gussied up for the game. A few of the players wanted to drop some things off in the locker room. Sauce was among the players who ventured into the building. Still filled with strong emotions, she decided to take a brief detour into the gym. Though it was empty, it wasn't completely dark. A few small lights in the corners of the gym cast enough of a glow that Sauce was able to make out the banners on the wall.

As she stared at the girls basketball banner, her mind transported her 20 years into the future. She imagined bringing her own daughter to a game, and as they sat together in the stands, Sauce could tell the story of the buzzer-beater she made to win the conference championship. Then she would point proudly to the first entry on the bottom half of the banner, where it listed state tournament appearances and say to her daughter, "That was us.

After 45 years of failing to make the state tournament, our team was the first."

Unlike the girls, the Waconia boys basketball team had not shifted to a new section during the realignment in the spring. That meant it was an easy 14-mile drive for the girls to get to Chanhassen to see the section championship. Many of the fans who had cheered on the girls that afternoon had also come to support the boys. Easily identified in their platinum-colored state tournament sweatshirts, the girls felt like celebrities as they walked through the crowd on their way to the student section. It took a long time to reach their seats as familiar faces and people they had never met all offered their congratulations on a great season. Several spectators made it a point to proclaim how proud they were of the team.

Shortly before halftime, athletic director Jill Johnson approached the student section and instructed the girls not to go anywhere. Johnson stood close by to ensure that none of the girls got a head start on a bathroom break or snuck away to get a snack from the concession stand.

When the first half came to a close and the boys teams left for the locker rooms, the public address announcer asked for the fans' attention. "This afternoon the Waconia girls basketball team's historic season ended with a loss in the Class AAA semifinals. This remarkable group of girls accomplished what no Waconia team in all the years before them ever had. These ladies were the first Waconia girls basketball team *ever* to reach the state tournament. At this time, we would ask for the members of the team to come out to halfcourt to be recognized."

Fans of both teams rose to their feet and applauded as the Wildcats made their way to halfcourt.

One year earlier, on that same floor, Snake, Sauce, and the rest of the Wildcats had their hearts broken. In that very spot, they were left crying and inconsolable, resigned to a red runner-up ribbon. Despite difficult times and dark moments in the 52 weeks that followed, hundreds of hours of hard work, enormous sacrifice, and a relentless persistence had brought them back.

Now, as a crowd of thousands stood in ovation, the Wildcats wore expressions of pride knowing they had accomplished their mission. They had made history. The angst they had experienced over the past year was absent, replaced with the comfort of knowing they would live the rest of their lives on the other side of glory.

Afterword:
Section Champs

When the season ended, it was announced that Snake was 1 of 10 players voted first-team All-State by the 64 coaches in Class AAA. Raptor and Scrunchie were recognized as All-State honorable mentions.

Two months after the state tournament, Salsa signed a scholarship to continue her basketball career at Division I Iona College in New Rochelle, New York.

Snake went on to play at the University of Wisconsin–Stout, where she majored in business.

Bird attended Winona State University and pursued a degree in veterinary medicine.

Will went to North Dakota State University and majored in criminal justice. She also indicated she hoped to get into coaching.

Sauce accepted an academic scholarship to attend the University of Wisconsin–Madison, where she majored in biology premed with the intent of becoming a physician specializing in dermatology.

By the end of the school year, Dusty "found" the 20 pounds he lost during the season.

Acknowledgments

Coach Neibauer and the entire roster of the Waconia girls basketball team were so giving through the writing process. They were giving of their time, responding to emails and text messages at all hours. They were also giving of themselves, willing to reveal their thoughts and feelings at different junctures of the season. It is obvious this book could not have happened without their complete cooperation. Thank you to everyone associated with the team.

I would also like to extend a heartfelt thank-you to my wife and our two sons. Even when I was physically home, I was too often absent during the years when I coached basketball, my mind consumed with an upcoming opponent or mulling ways I could make our team better. There is no doubt my retirement from coaching has made me a better husband and father, but there were times during the writing process when I reverted to the tunnel-vision focus that was a trademark of my coaching days. I will forever appreciate my family's patience and support while I worked on this book.

Finally, I want to thank my former high school basketball coach, Gary Munsen. Coach Munsen allowed me to be a part of a state championship basketball team even though I was a less-than-skilled player. Without him extending me that opportunity, I never would have enjoyed 20 years as a basketball coach. I never would have had the profound good fortune of coming to know the hundreds of fantastic kids, families, and coaches who have become such an important part of my life. If it weren't for Coach Munsen, I never would have been in a position to write this book. Thanks, Coach. You are missed every day.